D1590396

City of Refuge

City of Refuge

Slavery and Petit Marronage in the Great Dismal Swamp, 1763–1856

MARCUS P. NEVIUS

The University of Georgia Press
ATHENS

Most University of Georgia Press titles are
available from popular e-book vendors.

Printed digitally

Library of Congress Cataloging-in-Publication Data

NAMES: Nevius, Marcus P. (Marcus Peyton), 1983– author.
TITLE: City of refuge : slavery and petit marronage in the Great Dismal Swamp,
    1763–1856 / Marcus P. Nevius.
OTHER TITLES: Race in the Atlantic world, 1700–1900.
DESCRIPTION: Athens : The University of Georgia Press, [2020] | Series: Race in
    the Atlantic world, 1700-1900 | Includes bibliographical references and index.
IDENTIFIERS: LCCN 2019026474 | ISBN 9780820356426 (hardcover) |
    ISBN 9780820356419 (ebook)
SUBJECTS: LCSH: Fugitive slaves—Dismal Swamp (N.C. and Va.)—History.
    | Fugitive slave communities—Dismal Swamp (N.C. and Va.)—History.
    | Maroons—Dismal Swamp (N.C. and Va.)—History. | Slaves—Dismal
    Swamp (N.C. and Va.)—History. | Dismal Swamp (N.C. and Va.)—History.
CLASSIFICATION: LCC E445.N8 N48 2020 | DDC 306.3/6209755523—dc23
LC record available at https://lccn.loc.gov/2019026474

To Bernice and Hank Jennings Jr.,
mother and father to the Jennings clan:
gone in the physical form
but ever with us in our hearts.

CONTENTS

FIGURES

ACKNOWLEDGMENTS

Before a book project moves forward to print, a historian engages a moment that signals a transition from active efforts to compile archival records and historical volumes to drafting and redrafting essays and chapters and finally to a period of active reflection regarding these pursuits. I am truly thankful to the many people who have encouraged me to become knowledgeable about the histories of slave resistance, of marronage, and of informal slave economies in the early United States and the Atlantic world. I am grateful to the staff and faculties of a number of archives, libraries, and institutions: the North Carolina Collection and the Southern Historical Collection at Wilson Library at the University of North Carolina at Chapel Hill; the David M. Rubenstein Rare Book and Manuscript Library and Perkins Library at Duke University; the State Archives of North Carolina; the Alderman Library Special Collections (now the Albert and Shirley Small Special Collections Library) at the University of Virginia; the Special Collections at Swem Library at the College of William and Mary; the Virginia Historical Society (now the Virginia Museum of History and Culture); the Library of Virginia; and the Norfolk County Historical Society at the Chesapeake Public Library, Chesapeake, Virginia. For assistance in tracking down information about Edmund Jackson, I owe a deep debt of gratitude to Elizabeth Pope of the American Antiquarian Society and to Elizabeth Stevens of the Rhode Island Historical Society.

I have been very fortunate to receive significant research support for this project. The Department of History at the Ohio State University awarded me a number of travel and research grants: the Diversity Travel grant, the Summer Research Award, and the Henry H. Simms Award, and the College of Arts and Sciences (CAS) awarded several research grants to support this project during the dissertation phase. A history department Retrieving the American Past Research Award funded my participation in the 2013 Great Dismal Swamp Landscape Study Archaeology Field School (GDSLS), led by Daniel O. Sayers of American University. In Ohio, Alan Gallay and Noeleen McIlvenna vouched for me as I applied to join Dan's field school, and during five weeks of study in Virginia, I became a more well rounded scholar in conversations with Kathryn Benjamin Golden, Mark Hamilton, Julia Klima, and Daniel Lynch. A Mellon Fellowship, awarded by the Virginia Historical Society in 2015, funded my research of Richard Blow's letterbooks. During my time at the society, John McClure and Francis S. Pollard welcomed me warmly, and even encouraged me to sit for an interview that appeared in the VHS's History Notes magazine in Fall 2015. At the University of Rhode Island (URI), history department and Africana Studies program professional development travel funding and the Richard Beaupre Hope and Heritage award granted by the CAS have supported this project. For this support, I am particularly grateful to the university provost, Donald DeHayes; to the former CAS dean, Winifred Brownell; to the current CAS dean, Jeannette Riley; to the former chair of the Africana Studies program, Vanessa Quainoo; to the recent program chair, Bob Dilworth; and to the Department of History chair, Rod Mather. I am also grateful to Annu Palakunnathu Matthew and the board members of the URI Center for the Humanities for a Faculty Research Grant awarded in 2017 as well as for the Mark and Donna Ross faculty subvention grant in 2019 that aided my efforts to finish the manuscript.

Over the past decade, a number of audiences have made vital contributions to my efforts to frame *City of Refuge*. In 2017, Fran Botkin and Paul Youngquist coordinated a wonderful meeting of the ninth Charles Town International Maroon Conference, during which I received the wisdom offered by the descendants of the Windward Maroons in Portland Parish, Jamaica. In the same year, the Newport Middle Passage Port Markers Project and Canning Church Learning Center welcomed me warmly as I gave a talk about the hidden and thriving communities of escaped slaves who claimed space in the Dismal. Joanne Pope Melish told me about Brown University's Nineteenth Century U.S. History Workshop, and I am grateful that Seth Rockman invited me to lead a February 2018 meeting of the seminar, after which Linford Fisher encouraged me to think even more carefully about how I might concisely frame the Dismal's Native American history in this book's early pages. Josh Piker, Karin Wulf, and several others raised good questions that helped me to think through Edmund Boothe's story of freedom and unfreedom during the 2018 meeting of the Virginia Consortium of Early Americanists. During the 2018 meeting of the Caribbean Studies Association in Havana, conversations with Robert Connell, Sarah Jessica Johnson, and Alex Moulton greatly enriched my understanding of marronage with regard to recent studies in politics and the environment, literature, and geography. I have also received good feedback at graduate student history conferences at Duke University, Louisiana State University, and North Carolina State University.

Worthy of special mention are the important questions that two scholars—Shepherd W. McKinley and Sally E. Hadden—offered at two conferences in 2012. Their inquiries and curiosities regarding the meanings of marronage to enslaved people and to white Virginians and North Carolinians and the concepts of autonomy, parallel spaces, and collective consciousness were indispensable to my work in its early stages. In particular, Hadden's advice to "follow the money" launched several lines of inquiry that are not manifest in the pages to follow. Early iterations of *City of Refuge* also found keen audiences at the 2017 meeting of the Underground Railroad Conference; and during several meetings of the Association for the Study of African American Life and History.

I have been fortunate to receive guidance from scholars whose works have shaped my own. The late Bob Engs of the University of Pennsylvania and the College of William and Mary encouraged my interests in history even as he assailed my prose as the work of an "illiterate Etruscan." My master's thesis adviser at North Carolina Central University, Freddie L. Parker, published two books that first inspired me to tell the stories of the men, women, and children who "lurked about the neighbourhood." My master thesis's committee members, Jim C. Harper and Joshua Nadel, offered sage advice during the earliest stages of this project. My peers, including TaKeia Anthony, James Blackwell, A. J. Donaldson, D'Weston Haywood, and Brandon Winford often served as captive audiences for my ideas. Once I began my doctoral studies at Ohio State, North Carolina Central faculty Tony Frazier, Jerry Gershenhorn, Lydia Lindsey, and Carlton Wilson eagerly followed my progress. In Columbus, Curtis Austin, Hasan Kwame Jeffries, Stephanie Shaw, Tyran Steward, and William Sturkey exemplified the scholarly standards I have since sought to emulate in my own work. Dani Anthony, John Brown, Sarajaneé Davis, Jamie Goodall, Tim Leech, Cam Shriver, and Jessica Wallace encouraged me to remain steadfast in my pursuit of the Great Dismal's maroons. Mark Boonshoft and Kevin Vrevich graciously sifted through rough chapter drafts, offered insightful suggestions, raised interesting and challenging questions, and pointed to key works that I might engage in my own studies. My dissertation committee members, Kenneth Goings and Margaret Newell, have remained interested in and supportive of my scholarly ambitions. "Doc" Samuel Hodges seized the opportunity to serve as an external reader of my dissertation. My adviser, Leslie Alexander, has long been a champion of my studies and of my career.

In the spring of 2016, Ruth Dunnell, chair of the Department of History at Kenyon College, offered me a visiting position that supported my efforts to finish my dissertation. Glenn McNair, then on sabbatical, graciously offered his office as a home for my studies; Patrick Bottinger, Jeff Bowman, Jené Schoenfield, Sylvie Coulibaly, and Ennis Edmonds warmly welcomed me to Gambier. Since the fall of 2016, I have enjoyed the fortune of being a faculty member in perhaps the most collegial department at URI, the Department of History. My colleagues have offered advice and encouragement that has aided my transition from graduate student to faculty member. For this support I am ever grateful to Kate Bush, Bridget Buxton, Cathy DeCesare, Rae Ferguson, Tim George, Christian Gonzales, Michael Honhart, Erik Loomis, Rosie Maria Pegueros, Joëlle Rollo-Koster, Eve Sterne, Alan Verskin, James Mace Ward, and Rob Widell. As a CAS faculty mentor, Kendall Moore has been kind and patient, warm and welcoming. I have also benefited immensely from the advice and fellowship of my colleagues in Africana Studies, particularly Norman Barber, Gitahi Gititi, Shanette Harris, and John McCray. I am deeply grateful for Chris Hunter and the members of the Faculty and Staff Association of the African Diaspora including Earl Smith and Gerald Williams, who facilitate a vital organization that creates space for fellowship in the diaspora on campus.

Walter Biggins encouraged me to submit a manuscript based on my dissertation for publication by the University of Georgia Press. The press's external readers offered crucial advice that helped me to find my scholarly voice. Beth Snead, Jon Davies, and the editorial staff at the press expertly shepherded this manuscript through the publishing process, and Ellen Goldlust carefully refined my scholarly voice with keen copyedits. The members of the editorial board of the Race in the Atlantic World Series showed an interest in and approval of this project that speaks volumes about the importance of slave resistance and marronage in the history of the Atlantic world.

My family has supported my decade-long journey in scholarship. My father-in-law, Barry Gales, has expressed confidence in this project from our first conversation. My mother- and aunt-in-law, Julia Gales and Diane De Los Santos, have regularly expressed their interest in a story that involves the state that was home to many of their ancestors, Virginia. My brother,

Garrett, may seem to care less about this work, but I know that even he secretly enjoys the pursuits of a scholar. My dad, Gary Nevius, regularly offers his gregarious laugh and reminds me to remain focused. My mother, Wini Jennings, and stepfather, Philip Sutton, have tolerated this journey and encouraged me every step of the way even as they worried about where I might land next. At family gatherings, my maternal aunts and uncles—especially Aunt Cynthia—have expressed pride in our family's "doctor." They remind me that my late grandparents, Bernice and Henry E. Jennings Jr., are with me in spirit in this work. I know that I carry forward the legacy that my grandfather, a pillar of New Brunswick's African American community, established as a proud lecturer among New Jersey's Prince Hall Master Masons. The sense of accomplishment that comes along with finishing a book is powerful to be sure, but it is placed into broader perspective when I reflect on what it means to be of the Jennings clan, what it means to be of New Brunswick.

Of all the support I have enjoyed, by far the most steadfast love and encouragement have come from my partner and wife, Jihan. For the past decade, she has stood by me even as this work has meant that we have traveled the scenic route in this journey we call our life together. I am eternally grateful for her support and sacrifices. I know that she is just as happy as I am (if not more so) to see this project come to print. Jihan, you are my heart, now and forever.

City of Refuge

INTRODUCTION

In January 1852, Edmund Jackson, a wealthy abolitionist and merchant, published an essay, "The Virginia Maroons" in the *Liberty Bell*, a journal distributed in Boston's antislavery networks from 1839 to 1857.[1] In the 1840s, Jackson had been an active critic of segregation in Boston's public school system, and he had written pieces that highlighted slave flight as self-emancipation and condemned the vigor with which authorities, acting as agents, pursued runaways.[2] Having visited Virginia in 1819 to observe Mount Vernon twenty years after George Washington's death, Jackson described having heard about enslaved people being compelled to labor in the Great Dismal Swamp several miles south of Norfolk, Virginia's key Atlantic port at the lower end of the Chesapeake. To resist enslavement, the Dismal's slaves often fled the timber camps to claim spaces in the swamp's most remote regions. A "city of refuge in the midst of Slavery," these fugitive camps were "small communities" not unlike maroon colonies in Hispaniola, Cuba, and Jamaica, where enslaved Africans as far back as the sixteenth century had fled colonial settlements to form communities of resistance and freedom. Thus, while Jackson's previous works framed slave flight within the traditional lenses of fugitivity in the United States, "The Virginia Maroons" departed from these tropes to cast the subject in the context of slave resistance in the broader Atlantic world.[3]

Enslaved Africans had sought refuge in the interior mountainous regions of Hispaniola and in the heavily forested interior regions of Cuba, yet the most famous of these Caribbean spaces were the maroon communities that formed in Jamaica in the late seventeenth and early eighteenth centuries. The Jamaican maroons became widely known in reports that detailed skirmishes with British colonial troops during two wars. The First Maroon

War began in 1728 and ended with treaties signed by Captain Cudjoe of the Leeward maroons in 1739 and Queen Nanny of the Windward maroons in 1740 that facilitated a tenuous peace between the maroons and British colonial officials. Thereafter, colonial officials saw the maroons as autonomous communities whose presence helped to secure the island against slave flight or occupation by competing European states. The pacts established maroon land claims in the western and eastern Jamaican highlands, creating sovereign communities governed by maroon leaders whose presence undermined concurrent ideologies of enslaver supremacy that undergirded violent systems of discipline on sugar plantations in Jamaica and on other Caribbean islands.[4]

In Jamaica, this tenuous peace between maroons and colonial militias ruptured during the Second Maroon War (1795–96), which resulted in the forced deportation of the residents of Cudjoe Town (known as Trelawny Town at the time) and coincided with early nineteenth-century reports of marronage in the French, Spanish, and Dutch Caribbean.[5] By the 1840s, the currents of information exchange among correspondents in Atlantic world ports as far-flung as Boston, Norfolk, and Kingston ensured that Jackson knew about slave revolts and marronage in the Caribbean.[6] Others among Jackson's contemporaries similarly found inspiration in the reports of maroons in the Dismal. Between December 1855 and September 1856, Harriet Beecher Stowe published *Dred: A Tale of the Great Dismal Swamp*, a novel whose title character was a fictional son of Denmark Vesey, the leader of the attempted 1822 insurrection in Charleston, South Carolina.[7] Dred lived in a Dismal Swamp maroon community known only to enslaved people in the region. But the marronage specter that Stowe enlisted to bring Dred's world to life depicted a truth commonly known to local black and white residents. In the same year that *Dred* was published, David Hunter Strother, a travelogue author and illustrator, toured a Dismal lumber site, Horse Camp, accompanied by two enslaved boatmen who plied the swamp's canals with the forest products wrested from its landscape by enslaved laborers. Departing a causeway, Strother ventured a short distance into the dense undergrowth. Halting when he heard footsteps, Strother encountered a man he described as a "gigantic negro, with a tattered blanket wrapped about his shoulders, and a gun in his hand." The man was dressed in "a pair of ragged breeches and boots," with physical features that Strother viewed as "purely African." Although the man was strong and physically imposing, Strother was surprised by his apprehensive posture. Choosing not to engage the man, Strother returned to the causeway, where he sketched the man. The enslaved boatmen identified the man as "Osman" but answered no more of Strother's questions.[8]

For millennia before the 1860s, the Great Dismal Swamp was a vast natural wetland that covered nearly 2,000 square miles along the border of Virginia and North Carolina, a land area comparable to the modern state of Delaware. Various enterprises drained Great Dismal to a tenth of its original land area after the American Civil War, as growing postbellum industrial enterprises targeted forests in the U.S. Southeast.[9] Currently comprising two wildlife preserves overseen by two government agencies, the larger swamp sector covers an area of about 175 square miles, preserved by the U.S. Fish and Wildlife Service as the Great Dismal Swamp National Wildlife Refuge. A smaller sector along the Great Dismal Swamp Canal in Camden County, North Carolina, comprises almost 14,500 acres maintained by the state as the Dismal Swamp State Park. Near the swamp's center is Lake Drummond, a circular natural body of freshwater that covers more than 3,000 acres and is no more than six feet deep. Throughout the present-day swamp, old canals and drainage ditches carry still waters covered in algae, most clogged with swamp undergrowth after years of lying fallow. The Dismal's low-hanging tree limbs and dense underbrush frame the swamp's fringes, verdant in the warmer months of the year, dry and foreboding in the colder months. In some swamp sectors, a range of tree species—Atlantic white cypress, bald cypress, maple, and pine—rise from the swamp floor, spreading their branches and leaves high above. In other swamp sectors, the trees have been burned away by the regular natural fires sparked by lightning during frequent spring and summer storms. The swamp's interior features a damp floor of vegetation covered in leaf litter and fallen branches in some places, muddy under foot and covered with layers of peat in other places, and with shallow, dark-amber-colored standing water in still other places.

Small islands of dry landscape, known locally as hummocks, rise above the water table to heights of no more than ten feet. The hummocks are home to black bears, bobcats, otters, beavers, and squirrels. Colorful skinks and venomous snakes lie camouflaged on hummock floors where the sun's rays break through the forest canopy. The hummocks are also home to mosquitoes and yellow flies, voracious in their appetites for host animals and people. The Dismal's primary historical archaeologist, Daniel O. Sayers,

[handwritten margin note: As big as DE]

has led teams that have uncovered thousands of material artifacts on these hummocks and in other swamp locations. The artifacts include stone tools and lithic sherds that suggest such tools were reworked, low-fired ceramics, green shards of bottle glass, nineteenth-century cut nails, fire pits, and post-in-ground footprints. Sayers and his teams have found that the distribution of seventeenth-century Native American artifacts in swamp soils suggests that later generations of maroons who claimed space in the swamp recovered and modified older materials, including stone tools and projectile points.[10] Archaeologist Becca Peixotto has uncovered more than two thousand artifacts at two sites near the Dismal Swamp Canal, and archaeologist Cynthia V. Goode has excavated sites at Dismal Town and Jericho Ditch, uncovering similar artifacts that provide evidence of the distinctive "foodways, medicine, and household" lives of enslaved swamp laborers "under different work conditions and labor organization."[11]

These material artifacts bolster historical documentary evidence of the swamp's stories of petit marronage, of informal economies of exchange between enslaved African Americans and fugitives, and of the region's extractive economies. Before the end of the Tuscarora War in 1713, Algonquian-speaking Powhatan traders crossed the Dismal to exchange goods with Siouan-speaking Occaneechees to the west of the Piedmont riverine fall line. Powhatan traders also engaged with Iroquoian-speaking Nottoways, Meherrins, and Tuscaroras, all of whom lived along the swamp's southern fringe.[12] As permanent English colonization expanded westward from the Atlantic coast during the seventeenth century, the traditional homeland of the Powhatan Confederacy became the tidewater tobacco plantations on which Virginia planters enslaved hundreds of Africans and their descendants.

Tidewater and piedmont land claimed by land speculators became subject to squatting by members of the lower ranks of Virginia's expanding slave society. Even in the mid-eighteenth century, as provincial agricultural societies matured into slave societies, the Dismal remained largely unaltered, a potential refuge for enslaved Africans. As Virginia governor William Gooch reported to the British Board of Trade in September 1730, enslaved Africans were known to have met in groups "in several Parts of the Country" near the Dismal to plan a rebellion, inspired by the rumor that former governor Alexander Spotswood had decreed that enslaved people would be emancipated when they converted to Christianity. The ensuing Chesapeake Rebellion was the largest slave uprising during the British North American colonial era, though it did not succeed. Nevertheless, another contemporary observer, naturalist John Brickell, reported that two hundred Africans escaped to the Dismal's hummocks in the revolt's wake.[13]

Though little documented in archival evidence beyond Brickell's observations, the Africans of the Chesapeake Rebellion became the first significant population of slaves to seek refuge in the Dismal. By the mid-eighteenth century, land-speculating Virginians targeted the Dismal in plantation enterprise drainage schemes. Conceived as early as 1728 by William Byrd II, this effort began with the establishment of the Dismal Swamp Company in 1763 and the construction of Dismal Plantation at Dismal Town, near the swamp's northwestern fringe, two years later. In tracing this story, *City of Refuge* also traces a social history of white company agents and officials who exploited enslaved labor to service Atlantic markets near and far. To populate the Dismal's slave labor camps, local land and canal companies "hired" enslaved people via annual contracts that documented agreements between company officials and local enslavers. These contracts transferred temporary ownership of an enslaved person to the Dismal's land and canal companies and bound companies to specific responsibilities. Historian John J. Zaborney has observed that after the American Revolution, this system of slave hire increasingly reflected a new and complex form of flexibility in the slave societies of the Lower Chesapeake. Slave hiring thus became integral to slaveholders' efforts to maintain and to expand slavery in the region.[14]

Until the mid-1810s, the Dismal Swamp Company appointed agents to establish and expand Dismal Plantation as an agricultural enterprise. However, these agents failed to compel enslaved people at Dismal Plantation to efficiently produce rice and grain and gradually directed company slaves to cut and to mill the swamp's trees. This enterprise was ultimately reincorporated as the Dismal Swamp Land Company, which continued to hire local enslaved people through the antebellum period and operated until 1871. Slave hiring became more difficult after 1800, as enslaved Virginians were auctioned in increasing numbers to domestic slave traders in Norfolk or Richmond before being forcibly transported to New Orleans, the central slave market in the new Southwest.[15] Other Virginians sought to remove enslaved people to the west coast of Africa, an effort formalized with the 1816 establishment of the American Colonization Society.[16] With local enslavers unable to meet the land and canal companies' labor requirements, company agents tapped what historian and archaeologist Ted Maris-Wolf has described as the Dismal's maroon "communities within communities." Hidden in the center of a swamp that itself was characterized by a particularly unique context of a "biracial labor system that relied upon and supported slavery," the Dismal's land and canal companies sought maroons as a key source of labor, alongside the hundreds of enslaved people the companies dispatched to timber camps.[17]

For more than a century, the Dismal's maroon communities were less a permanent population and more multiple semipermanent settlements that shared the common goal of a meaningful existence during extended time encamped in the swamp. In their interactions with enslaved people at the swamp's scattered slave labor camps, the Dismal's maroons also retained some important connections to the surrounding slave societies. In the 1850s, then, Strother likely encountered in Osman an American maroon who lived deeper in the swamp. Osman might have provided enslaved shinglers at Horse Camp with timber that he had cut on his own or with a group of maroons in exchange for clothing, weaponry, and other rations. Such exchanges were common, though they usually occurred via informal arrangements that were rarely recorded by the land and canal companies. To this end, Osman's emergence from beyond the pale of the Dismal's trees teases another theme that *City of Refuge* traces: the internal exchange economy involving enslaved people, maroons, and white canal and land company agents. This system was akin to internal economies that sustained fugitive slaves in other Virginia contexts and beyond.[18] Osman's worldly possessions—the blanket and gun—exemplified the investments that land company shareholders made to compel the Dismal's slaves to labor in the service of company profits in markets both near and far. By the 1830s, hundreds of enslaved canal cutters, shingle getters and porters, and letter carriers animated the land and canal companies' operations in a pattern that ebbed and flowed with broader national and global economic trends over the following two decades. These efforts gave Osman's Dismal Swamp the character by which a broad spectrum of abolitionists and slavery critics—among them Frederick Douglass, Edmund Jackson, David Hunter Strother, and Harriet Beecher Stowe—sought to reach the readers of abolitionist tracts, journals, newspapers, and novels.

Maroon camps and communities formed in the southeastern United States; in the islands of the British, Spanish, Dutch, and French Caribbean; and in Central and South America. A verb, the general term "marronage" derives from the Spanish term *cimarrón*, first used in Hispaniola in reference to feral cattle in the 1530s. Later in the century, Spanish colonizers used *cimarrón* to refer to the actions of enslaved indigenous people who fled to the hinterlands of local Spanish colonies. By the seventeenth century, the English adapted the term "maroon" and the French and Dutch adapted the term "marron" in reference to enslaved absconders. In the early nineteenth century, U.S. officials used the term "Seminole" to describe slave flight into the Florida panhandle.[19] Since the 1970s, scholars have debated the definition of marronage in two contexts: grand marronage and petit marronage. Enslaved individuals or small groups of enslaved people engaged in petit marronage fled oppressive slave societies in the short term, without intending to remain indefinitely in flight or to escape permanently from the region in which they lived. The largest maroon camps reflected grand marronage, communities that penetrated the foundations of plantation systems throughout the Atlantic world, as anthropologist Richard Price, an early authority on the subject of marronage, has explained.[20]

Scholarly interest in what might be termed "American marronage" dates to World War II–era scholarly debates on the contours of slavery in the Western Hemisphere. Pointing to an Atlantic context for African enslavement, historians, including Eric Williams (later the first prime minister of Trinidad and Tobago), pointed to the centrality of the African slave trade in British economic development.[21] Scholars including Philip Curtin compiled the records of transatlantic slaving voyages, creating an archive of the Middle Passage that generated significant debates that determined that more than ten million Africans were forcibly transported across the Atlantic.[22] Engaged in debate with reconciliationist historians who cast enslaved people as docile and inferior to whites, historians John Hope Franklin and Herbert Aptheker pointed to marronage as the foremost example of slave resistance on a spectrum ranging from outright rebellion to individual acts including arson, poisoning enslavers, and truancy.[23]

By the mid-twentieth century, scholars debated the degree to which slavery had been the central problem of American and southern legal, cultural, institutional, and intellectual thought and custom.[24] From the mid-1970s to the first decade of the twenty-first century, historians—most notably the late Ira Berlin, the late David Brion Davis, Edmund Morgan, and Philip Morgan—produced voluminous bodies of work that traced the gradual developments in legal, economic, and societal institutions that shaped slave societies regionally and locally.[25] Still more recent studies have reminded scholars that American slavery was indeed national but was shaped by urban and rural contexts and both included and excluded significant populations of poor and middling whites.[26] In particular, scholars have argued convincingly that the problem of African American enslavement was central to the American independence struggle.[27] Historians Woody Holton, Michael A. McDonnell, and James Sidbury have noted that the interests of Native Americans, of enslaved people, of debtors, and of slaveholding elites in Virginia converged and diverged in important ways during the revolution, creating a "politics of war" that both Patriots and Loyalists sought to marshal.[28] Still other histories have considered closely the ways that enslaved Africans and Native Americans blurred lines of race and color, ethnicity, and sovereignty.[29] Studies by Kathleen Brown, Emily Clark, Jennifer Morgan, Rebecca Scott, Brenda Stevenson, and the late Stephanie M. H. Camp have also highlighted the central role of black women, enslaved and free, in slave resistance and in Atlantic world contexts.[30] Recent scholarship has also traced the histories of African American communities and identities, highlighting the central problem of slave resistance in the history of the United States and the Atlantic world.[31] Vincent Harding has observed slave resistance and community formation as a dynamic movement for justice in all aspects of life—a metaphorical river of struggle that was representative of the "transformative power that humans create" to sustain an indomitable hope.[32] Studies by Michael Gomez, Gerald Horne, Walter Rucker, and Jason Young have posed new directions for the history of black resistance, emphasizing African identities at the root of slave resistance.[33] Historians including Sharla Fett, Sowandé Mustakeem, Gregory O'Malley, and Stephanie Smallwood have more recently reexamined the Middle Passage to emphasize the vast scale of abject human commodification in the service of Atlantic slave markets.[34]

Even before the federal ban on the importation of enslaved people from Atlantic markets went into effect in 1808, legislators in Virginia and North Carolina debated the viability of transatlantic slave trading. In 1778, the Virginia General Assembly banned the importation of enslaved Africans from Africa or the West Indies. Four years earlier, the North Carolina Provincial Congress had banned the importation of enslaved Africans, setting a precedent for subsequent acts in 1786, 1794, and 1795.[35] By 1815, prominent Virginians and North Carolinians also sought to reduce rising free black populations by funding an organization that would facilitate removal to West Africa. The most famous of these colonization schemes were facilitated by the American Colonization Society, founded in December 1816 in Washington, D.C., with branches in Maryland, Virginia, and other states.[36] The transatlantic and domestic slave trades comprised the core problem of the nation's first seventy-eight years, an issue upon which antislavery activists and abolitionists seized in the effort to agitate politically and to shape public opinion.[37] Before the Civil War, American slavery became indisputably national, the result of compromises that undergirded political alliances at the federal and state levels between Whigs and Democratic Republicans from the late 1780s through the early 1810s and between aging Whigs, a younger generation of Republicans, and Democrats for the next three-plus decades. This nationalization resulted from significant advances in plantation technologies, the expansion of the financial networks that infused capital—domestic and especially foreign—into new slave societies in the Deep South, and abolitionists' work to make the abstraction of a geographically distant slave South the truth of a deeply entrenched Slave Power that controlled the levers of politics and of industrial economies at the federal and state levels across the country.[38]

Historians including Edward Baptist, Daina Ramey Berry, Joshua D. Rothman, and Calvin Schermerhorn have observed that enslaved people forced to migrate southward were recorded often in new plantation ledgers as "hands," a term that deemphasized humanity, even as enslaved Virginians and North Carolinians remained the human beings who bore the direct violence through which cotton planter agency was defined.[39] Historian Walter Johnson has observed that cotton planters' agency in the Lower Mississippi River Valley took shape at the intersection of ecology, agriculture, mastery, and economy, each governed by weather patterns, crop cycles, labor routines, market cycles, and the financial obligations that facilitated speculators' expansion into the North American continental interior. Key durable abstractions have long framed African American history through the contours of the master-slave relationship debates that sought to describe the measures of accommodation, negotiation, oppression, and repression that enslavers experienced in relation to enslaved people; through the role of white supremacy in forming American slave societies; and through the role of black resistance in acting as a check on these factors. In particular, Johnson observes that scholarly debates around slave agency have been "indispensable," but scholarly definitions of agency itself have also become "unmoored from the historical experiences" of enslaved people who resisted slavery in various temporal, regional, and specific contexts. Framed as the counter to the power that enslavers wielded over enslaved people and slave societies as a whole, agency has become a two-dimensional ideal that flattens the historical, temporal, and location-specific conditions that gave shape to black agency and resistance.[40]

Historians Sven Beckert and Seth Rockman observe that the scholarly consensus that slavery was "indispensable" to the economic development of the United States is simultaneously "self-evidently true and empirically obscure."[41] Taking these observations as a point of departure, *City of Refuge* engages in new ways the voluminous scholarship on slavery and capitalism, black resistance, and black agency in Virginia and North Carolina as well as in the Atlantic world more broadly. Historian Nathaniel Millett has argued that most evidence of North American marronage reflects "desperate bands of runaways" who struggled to survive each day, and the "Negro Fort" constructed in the 1810s at Prospect Bluff in British territory along the Apalachicola River in the Florida panhandle reflects the only instance of grand marronage in North America. During the Civil War, Thomas Wentworth Higginson, the leading officer of the first black military unit, the First South Carolina Volunteers, pondered whether his choice to lead an all-black regiment would lead to his branding as an outlaw leader of maroons. Higginson's anxiety was rooted in knowledge of a "cutting edge version of freedom" exemplified in the convergence of "exceptional geopolitics, tradition," and the unique circumstances of growing antislavery in the British empire that took shape in the borderlands of the Florida panhandle. How Prospect Bluff's "former slaves constructed their freedom," Millett argues, is remarkable—a lens through which slave consciousness and the extent of the black freedom struggle might come into sharper focus.[42]

Only under rare conditions could large-scale maroon encampments, including the one at Prospect Bluff, take shape in North America. Far more common were the conditions under which enslaved Africans and African Americans engaged in petit marronage, resisting enslavement in smaller-scale, highly mobile camps. These camps, too, provide an important lens through which the extent of the black freedom struggle is brought into sharper focus. Historian Sylviane A. Diouf has noted that the Dismal's maroon communities were distinctive in that they were established in two distinct zones, the interior hinterland and the borderlands along the edges. Documented only in limited primary sources, the Dismal's shingle getters comprised one key population of potential maroons, while enslaved people who fled local farms and plantations comprised a second population.[43] But although "American maroons"—to take Diouf's term—took refuge in the swamp, they gradually became confined to shrinking geographic spaces in the Dismal's deepest reaches.

The state with the largest U.S. slave population through 1860, Virginia offered a context for slavery that was a key focus of abolitionists' efforts to agitate for gradual and later immediate abolition. To 1840s abolitionists including Frederick Douglass, what distinguished the Dismal was not the question of marronage but the presence of "slaves in the Dismal swamp."[44] What, then, are we to make of what Jackson described as the Dismal's "city of refuge" for maroons—a setting that imagined interconnected but distinctly separate slave labor and maroon camps—whose strange history has long captivated scholars and readers of the histories of black resistance and agency? In answering these inquiries, *City of Refuge* reads the history of petit marronage the Great Dismal Swamp as a complex human history of slave agency and enslaved laborer guile in negotiating the oppressive terms of slavery in an extreme environment unlike the Chesapeake tobacco plantations of old or the cotton plantations of the new Southwest. In perhaps the purest sense, the Dismal's maroons were freedom's seekers who originated in plantation or swamp slave labor camp contexts and who engaged in petit marronage to repudiate altogether the slave societies that surrounded and encroached on the swamp.[45] For this reason, the Dismal's history of petit marronage cannot be decoupled from its histories of extractive and informal exchange economies. Taking its cue from historian Manisha Sinha's argument that black resistance is central to the history of abolition in the United States, *City of Refuge* foregrounds petit marronage's persistence in the Dismal's history, in part reading it as black resistance revealed in the records of slavery in the Great Dismal Swamp.[46] These histories placed into context, present a fuller picture of unfreedom and slave labor in the Dismal.

This book explains that the history of petit marronage in the Great Dismal is perhaps best interpreted to be the narrative of negotiations and accommodations that took shape in varying temporal contexts. This explanation provides a fuller contextualization of the history of black resistance in the swamp, but it also sheds light on little-researched exchanges between slaveholders and enslaved people in unbalanced relationships that offer a prime example of how unfreedom for slaves did not equate to absolute mastery by enslavers.[47] *City of Refuge* is based on primary sources that include runaway advertisements; planters' and merchants' records, inventories, letterbooks, and correspondence; the records and inventories of land companies; colonial, provincial, and state records; abolitionist pamphlets and broadsides; and slave narratives. Few of these sources were written by enslaved people themselves; and in seeking refuge in the Dismal's most remote sectors, maroons did not leave written records. Because the extant materials were drafted by officials engaged in facilitating the region's extractive economy, finding the Dismal's maroons requires reading against the grain of extant sources, a technique that follows in the recent path forged by historian Marisa J. Fuentes's study of archival silence in the history of women in colonial Barbados. Because marronage comprised a form of slave resistance through which runaways hid from detection, and because the enslaved people dispatched into land company forced labor camps also performed their labors off the grid, the maroons and enslaved laborers whose experiences this book attempts to reconstruct are read through crucial glimpses that reflect the ways by which the Dismal's enslaved people negotiated their lives.[48]

To emphasize the centrality of enslaved people and American maroons within the Dismal's extractive and informal slave economies, *City of Refuge* directly engages archival silence in historical primary sources. Each chapter of this book begins with a key source or event that foregrounds enslaved Virginians and North Carolinians in what becomes an extended examination of the ways that the Lower Chesapeake's extractive economy took shape over time. The prologue introduces the twinned problems of slave resistance and petit marronage in the eighteenth-century Dismal Swamp, challenges that resulted in provincial laws and customs intended to curtail enslaved peoples' movements in the Virginia and North Carolina hinterlands; however, lax enforcement meant that these measures had only minimal effect. Chapter 1 introduces the Dismal's story of land speculation through the establishment of the first base of swamp operations in the 1760s, Dismal Town, where a group of land speculators headlined by Virginia's rising generation of aspiring men, including George Washington, invested in a venture that would become the Dismal Swamp Company (DSC). Incorporated in 1765, the DSC established Dismal Plantation, a slave labor camp at Dismal Town, on the swamp's northwestern fringe near Suffolk. Before 1770, more than fifty enslaved men and women were forced to cut drainage ditches and to fell trees under the oversight of George Washington's brother, John Augustine Washington. Throughout the decade, the number of enslaved people at Dismal Plantation decreased, for reasons including slave flight into remote sectors of the swamp. As the first skirmishes of the American Revolution reached southern Virginia in late 1775, Dismal Plantation overseers Jacob Collee and Dempsey Smith regularly reported a property in disrepair and an enslaved population marooned in the swamp.

Chapter 2 takes up the Dismal's story of black resistance and petit marronage. The chapter highlights the well-known historical fact that enslavers' fears of slave flight and slave rebellion spiked in Virginia and North Carolina during the American Revolution as well as in the first years of the early republic, fears that were given voice in numerous runaway advertisements and other correspondence. These fears peaked after provincial Virginia governor John Murray, Lord Dunmore, recruited several hundred blacks to join the Ethiopian Regiment of British forces against the Virginia militia in 1775. By November of that year, British forces and Loyalists evacuated Virginia, taking with them several hundred members of the regiment. Several hundred other former regiment members entered the Dismal, becoming a second significant population of African-descended people who sought refuge there. In the last four decades of the eighteenth century, slave unrest also generated fears among enslavers in North Carolina. In the 1760s, enslaved people witnessed or gathered rumors of the colony's distinctive Regular movement, in which settlers in the western backcountry rose in revolt against the colony's governing eastern elite.[49] In the following two decades, skirmishes during the American Revolution inspired enslaved people to flee local plantations, patterns of flight that persisted into the 1790s.

Chapter 3 traces the ways that Dismal Swamp Company officials and agents tacitly accepted petit marronage from the 1790s to 1820s, looking the other way as they sought to establish the Lower Chesapeake's extractive economy. By the 1790s, the DSC moved its base of swamp operations from Dismal Town to Suffolk, on the swamp's northwestern fringe. As records penned by agents John Driver, Thomas Swepson, and Frederick Hall reveal, this move meant less direct oversight for slaves in the swamp and more space for petit marronage to take shape. The DSC also faced competition from other ad hoc companies that sought to access the swamp's trees. Perhaps the most prominent of these companies, however, was the Dismal Swamp Canal Company (DSCC), an enterprise that used slave labor to construct the largest of these waterways, the Dismal Swamp Canal. Key letters written between 1805 and 1815 by Samuel Proctor, employed first by the DSCC and later by the DSC, reveal important distinctions and continuities in the overall strategy to tacitly permit enslaved shinglers and canal cutters to engage in petit marronage and informal economies of exchange.

Slave labor in the Dismal was perilous and arduous. Extant records contain no shortage of evidence that enslaved people struggled under extreme environmental conditions. Chapter 4 begins with the narrative of Moses Grandy, who purchased his freedom by saving sums he earned in overwork in the context of the Dismal's extractive and internal economies, in the process negotiating betrayal by two separate enslavers. Grandy's experiences illustrate that the Dismal remained largely undeveloped. But by the late 1820s, the scale of the region's extractive economy became increasingly institutionalized in the slave hire contracts that canal and land companies signed with local enslavers. These changes ultimately hindered the formation of a large long-term maroon colony in the Great Dismal, but in earlier years, the conditions prevailing in the Dismal's extractive and internal economies provided the cover that shielded petit marronage from the view of white Virginians and North Carolinians. Chapter 5 opens with reports of the Southampton Rebellion of 1831, highlighting the false rumors that Nathaniel Turner and the Southampton rebels had taken refuge in the Dismal. The rebellion generated significant fears of slave revolt regionally and nationally, but DSC and DSCC officials and agents left little evidence of their own reactions to the rebellion. Instead, company agents in particular continued to facilitate the daily business of extracting the Dismal's natural resources, and agents regularly called on company officials to send into the swamp provisions that included pork and other foods as well as clothing, blankets, and other materials.

By the 1840s, the Dismal's context for American slavery became widely known among abolitionists in northern circles and was presented as evidence of slavery's expansion and versatility in the works of abolitionist newspaper editors, essayists, novelists, and lecturers including Douglass, Jackson, and Stowe. Observers such as Frederick Law Olmsted and David Hunter Strother also referenced this strange setting for slavery. As visitors to the Lower Chesapeake in the antebellum era, these observers cited the Dismal's context for black resistance and slavery in efforts to shape public opinion by defining the Dismal's context for slavery. The Dismal likely drew national interest because its extractive economy expanded considerably, a story that Chapter 6 traces. The higher numbers of enslaved laborers in the Dismal led local legislators to establish registries that were entered into county courthouse records. The story of Edmond Boothe, enslaved by North Carolina's Orapeake Canal Company, demonstrates how the Dismal offered refuge to some black Virginians and North Carolinians even as the nation's political coalition that abolitionists called the "Slave Power" ensured that only Civil War would end American slavery.

City of Refuge closes with a brief epilogue that has two principal aims: the first engages with recent applications of marronage as a political concept that scholars including Steven Hahn and Neil Roberts have posited; the second presents a final application for this model of historical research, tracing the postbellum narrative of ex-slave William H. Robinson, published in 1913.

"Lurking in Swamps, Woods, or Other Obscure Places"

Petit Marronage in Eastern Virginia and North Carolina in the Eighteenth Century

In 1730, the largest slave uprising in colonial Virginia history raised an alarm in several Southside counties. In early November, more than two hundred enslaved Africans led by Congolese Christians assembled in Norfolk and Princess Anne Counties, along the eastern fringe of the Great Dismal Swamp. Local militia quickly suppressed the revolt, but in its wake, a significant number of rebels escaped into the Dismal. Reprisals came swiftly, yet naturalist John Brickell reported that the presence of these African rebels threatened passage through the region. Twenty-four rebels were hanged in the woods, and five leaders were captured, tried, and hanged. The Norfolk and Princess Anne militias received orders to patrol two to three times a week to prevent slaves' night meetings. To suppress further rebellious activity and to prevent runaway slaves from escaping into the Dismal, Virginians recruited local Native American groups to capture African maroons.[1] But in the greater Dismal Swamp region, these efforts had only marginal success. In the late 1730s, Englishman J. F. D. Smyth described maroons hiding in the region as "perfectly safe" and as able to "elude the most diligent search of their pursuers."[2]

With the exception of a few recent studies, historians have characterized maroons as runaways whose stories all but ended with the publication of advertisements seeking their return—the moment at which they disappeared from further public records. That such absconders attempted and remained in defiant flight in 1730, however, suggests a resilience that extended beyond mere escape. Two years prior to the Chesapeake Rebellion, a wealthy Virginia planter, Colonel William Byrd II, led an effort to survey the Dismal for the purpose of delineating the boundary with North Carolina. Recording his experiences in a travel journal published as *The History of the Dividing Line betwixt Virginia and N. Carolina*, Byrd described the movements of the team he led westward from Currituck Sound to survey the southern expanse of the Great Dismal. Another team of surveyors cut through the heart of the swamp's cypress forests from the west, working their way east to meet Byrd's men on the swamp's western edge. In March 1728, half a mile beyond the edge of the swamp's forest line, Byrd's team encountered a mulatto family whose members explained that they were free. Byrd could not conceal his skepticism, noting that slaves were known to take shelter among poor white people in the region. Byrd assumed that the family's condition made it necessary for them to acquiesce to any coercive terms set by the region's whites, but as one scholar has observed, Byrd's skepticism belies a significant reality: what seemed to be a situation of exploitation was most likely an economic interdependence between whites and nonwhites, an arrangement that reflected the circumstances for many social relationships in southeastern Virginia and northeastern North Carolina.[3]

Although Byrd's team interacted with the mulatto family, the other team reported no instances of human contact as it hacked through the center of the swamp. However, the mulatto family likely bore witness to the small communities of British (mostly Scots-Irish) settlers that dated to the mid-seventeenth century and were located in the counties surrounding the swamp. More recently, the mulatto family had likely interacted with members of the Tuscarora who had not fled north to join the League of Six Nations with the Iroquois and who had settled along the southwestern edge of the Dismal.[4] Similar Native American communities known as the Nansemond Indians formed on the swamp's western fringe, the result of the cross-cultural exchanges between descendants of the Meherrin, Chowanoke, and Catawba. Southwestern Gates County, North Carolina, was home to the Scratch Hall people, a hardscrabble community of subsistence farmers known to have tawny complexions. Virginia and North Carolina provincials viewed the Scratch Hall people as clannish, secretive, and brutish beer drinkers whose customs ran counter to those in the small English hamlets that took shape in northeastern North Carolina. The Scratch Hall communities were accessible only via winding footpaths that represented an intentional affront to English or British authority. Local knowledge dictated caution in interactions with the Scratch Hall people, who were notoriously inhospitable and irreverent when contacted by English authorities or travelers. In historian Arwin D. Smallwood's view, many of these triracial communities endured despite the changing legality of cross-racial cooperation.[5] In 1729, the Albemarle region reverted to royal control with the revocation of the seventeenth-century Carolina colony proprietary charter. In the Great Dismal, this latest projection of British authority was little more than nominal. County courts had long been the Albemarle's primary institutions of legal power, empowered with full judicial and administrative authority to license ordinaries, to plan and direct the construction of roads, to build bridges and fund ferries, and to regulate the region's credit system. County courts also had authority to define enslaved people in flight as outlaws and to function as separate slave tribunals to adjudicate slave codes.[6]

To discourage runaway slaves, the Virginia House of Burgesses in 1705 passed "An Act Concerning Servants and Slaves," which defined enslavement as limited to persons of African descent. The slave code encouraged white Virginians "to take up runaways," with bounties paid in tobacco to persons who captured enslaved people.[7] North Carolina's governing bodies enacted similar restrictions on slave movements in 1715 and strengthened them in 1741 with a reward system to incentivize the return of fugitive absentees, outliers, or maroons. The law also established public gaols. Whites found guilty of aiding absconding blacks who subsequently helped return the runaway were subject to a penalty of twenty-five pounds. If the runaways were not returned, the penalties were far worse: whites who were "afterwards apprehended and convicted" of aiding a runaway who remained at large "shall, by the said Court, be severally adjudged and condemned as guilty of Felony, and shall suffer accordingly."[8] Some provisions of the code imply maroon activity and thus betray the level of concern with which whites addressed the problem of marronage in North Carolina. Chapter XXIV, sections XV–XLVII specifically prohibited the arming of slaves to hunt in forests and swamps and created the slave pass system. Section XLV decreed that fugitive runaways were subject to capture by slave hunters. Lawmakers carefully noted, "Many Times Slaves run away and lie out hid and lurking in Swamps, Woods, or other obscure places, killing Cattle and Hogs, and committing other Injuries to the Inhabitants of this Government"; in response, lawmakers encoded guidelines that directed whites to report maroon activity or known maroons to at least two local justices of the peace. To discourage this sort of petit marronage, legislators entered into the code a caveat:

outlawed slaves could turn themselves in to local authorities for punishment. In addition, North Carolina legislators included a clause that allowed slave runaways to return to enslavers prior to capture.[9]

Yet by midcentury, controlling slaves' penchant for revolt proved increasingly difficult. In 1767, the Wilmington, North Carolina, militia confronted approximately twenty "runaway slaves in a body arm'd." The militia did not report how long the group had been in flight, preoccupied instead by the perceived threat that they posed. The rise in revolutionary fervor caused by the American independence struggle exacerbated fears of slave revolt. In the summer of 1775, as reports of the siege of Boston circulated across North Carolina, local militias in Craven and Pitt Counties encountered a maroon group preparing to gather arms in advance of an insurrection. According to the Pitt County safety committee, the militia had pursued "a band of 250 slaves" for several days but had captured only a few. On July 8, according to the committee, the slave group planned to kill the families that had once enslaved them, burn local whites' homes, and then move into the "Back country," to meet with persons "armed by the Government for their Protection."[10] The absconders would then be free to form their own government. The Pitt County safety committee believed that the absconders had caught wind of the Regulator Rebellion.[11] In 1767 and again in 1775, when they were perhaps inspired by the American independence struggle, two maroon groups near Wilmington posed perceptible threats against the town's white residents. Although local patrollers prevented the 1775 insurrection, the threat was all too real: the captured runaways were found to be in possession of a considerable number of arms. Had they not been disbanded, local authorities believed, the rebels might have attacked the region's slave society or settled in the vast forested hinterland to the south. In all of these cases, local authorities sought to criminalize enslaved people who sought freedom through petit marronage.

The Revolutionary War reached Virginia's shores in the form of a squadron of British vessels off shore at Hampton, across from Norfolk, in October 1775. The ensuing battle between Virginia militia and British forces resulted in part from the actions of Joseph Harris, a mulatto man who had served as a slave pilot on the Chesapeake Bay. On October 27, Harris presented himself to Lord Dunmore, the colony's last royal governor, prepared to fight in the imperial effort to retain the colonies in exchange for his freedom. Not only did Harris's intimate knowledge of Virginia's waterways prove useful to the British squadron, but his example enticed more runaways: prior to Harris's death on July 19, 1776, more than four hundred former slaves sailed away from Virginia with the British.[12]

However, these members of Dunmore's Ethiopian Regiment soon found themselves in Canada or the Caribbean living under conditions that left them little better off than enslaved Virginians.[13] But many others who enlisted in Dunmore's regiment chose to take matters into their own hands by taking refuge in the Great Dismal Swamp, following the example of the Chesapeake rebels who had fled into the Dismal a generation earlier. These maroons had seen not only an opportunity to abscond but also an opportunity to lay claim to the swamp. For many white Virginians and North Carolinians, then, the presence of enslaved Africans moving about local forests and swamps not only stimulated a perceived potential for organized revolt but also threatened social stability.

From whites' perspective, the problem of petit marronage was more complex than simply the threat of slave rebellion. Petit marronage enabled African Americans to establish spaces in which they could develop their own societies. And enslaved people who engaged in petit marronage might serve as couriers of insurrectionary information, traveling from plantation to plantation to recruit potential rebels. Beyond the reach of local militia and county patrols, maroon colonies had the potential to develop into towns controlled solely by blacks.

Nevertheless, this possibility was short lived. Both Virginia and North Carolina deepened their commitment to black enslavement. Although petit marronage persisted until the Civil War, slaveholders invested in tobacco's second frontier in the North Carolina piedmont and in the rise of Richmond as a major tobacco processor devoted more time and resources to the establishment of farms and homesteads. In part as a consequence of these combined pressures, the space for marronage shrank significantly.

CHAPTER 1

"Liv'd by Himself in the Desert about 13 Years"

*Slaves, Shingles, and the Early
Companies of the Dismal Swamp*

In 1763, William Aichison and James Parker recorded the first of eighty-eight numbered pages bound in green vellum, a book that reveals the extent to which the two men's business connections spanned the Atlantic world between the year that the British emerged victorious in the wake of the French and Indian War and 1804, fifteen years after the ratified U.S. Constitution put into place the government of the new sovereign nation.[1] Aichison and Parker's clients included local merchants William MacCormick and Company, operating in North Carolina, and John Lidderdale, operating in Williamsburg, Virginia. The two merchants' contacts also ranged beyond the Lower Chesapeake to Atlantic ports such as Havana, Cuba, and to Santa Cruz, in the Canary Islands. From Albert Nesbitt, their contact in Tenerife, the Norfolk merchants sought a shipment of "Canary brandy (if cheap)" along with "onions, Potatoes, Walnuts, Chestnuts, Raysons, Almonds," and figs. And Aichison and Parker had gathered items for transport to the Canaries, including pork (a Virginia staple), hog's lard, beeswax, flour, and sugar; they expected a cargo of "Indian Corn" to be readied for transport soon thereafter. In addition, the shipment included "Boards, 15 to 25 feet in length" and "Shingles & Clapboards for storehouses."[2]

Aichison and Parker had also agreed to deliver other cargo to Tenerife. Francisco Bentoso had consigned to them a cargo of pork and beef. Simon Herreras, Henrique Casalo, and Thomas Juan Russel had consigned horses to be delivered to the island. And for "Madam Russel," Aichison and Parker's ship would bring "2 Chests of drawers, of the upper of it for use of a table & the body to be divided into three drawers." Other entries reveal that Aichison and Parker also bore responsibility for transporting to Tenerife an enslaved girl "about 10 years old" and an enslaved thirty-five-year-old woman who understood "Cookery & Baking & is Cleanly, good tempered."[3]

That Aichison and Parker recorded nothing more about this woman reflects the violence of archival silence, a problem of historical methodology that until recently has limited the fullest narration of the histories of countless enslaved men, women, and children.[4] That the Norfolk merchants emphasized the woman's skills as a cook, along with her "good temper," reflects the ways that eighteenth- and nineteenth-century slaveholders reduced humans to arbitrary market values based on speculative assumptions tied to age, to temperament, to health, and to the prospective length of their lives as slave laborers, as historian Daina Ramey Berry has recently explained.[5] Such passing references, furthermore, are common in Atlantic world business ledgers. Another entry in the Aichison and Parker ledger references a local story of great interest. A "negroe man" had emerged from the "Dismal Swamp, or Deserts" after having "liv'd by himself in the Desert about 13 years." According to the merchants, the swamper explained that he had "raisd Rice & other grain" to sustain himself. But subsistence seemingly was not enough: the swamper claimed to have also produced "Chairs, Tables & musical instruments." The merchants did not mention the market for which the swamper produced his wares, apparently more intrigued that he had done so in a land that seemed mythical, serving as a refuge for "many Bears, Tigers, Raccoons" and a "great lake," Drummond's Pond.[6]

Given Aichison and Parker's interest in the "negroe man," it is possible that he produced the chest of drawers. Furthermore, Loyalists Aichison and Parker fled Virginia as Patriot resistance expanded in the war's earliest years, with James Parker's Norfolk mansion among the first to burn in January 1776.[7] Based solely on Aichison and Parker's ledger, the maroon furniture maker's experience seems fanciful. But set into the broader framing of the Dismal's extractive and informal slave economies, his tale becomes more plausible. In the 1730s, three decades before the two men began their ledger, the Great Dismal Swamp offered refuge to the Chesapeake rebels, Congolese Christians who had risen against Virginia's hardening slave society in Norfolk and Princess Anne Counties. The maroon furniture maker may have been one of the original enslaved people compelled to establish Dismal Plantation in the 1760s under the oversight of John Augustine Washington. The furniture maker might also have been among the rank and file of Lord Dunmore's Ethiopian Regiment who took refuge in the Dismal in late 1775.

With no further evidence regarding the furniture maker's existence, scholars face a deafening archival silence as they attempt to contextualize more broadly the human history of the Dismal Swamp in the late eighteenth century. Among the key questions that frame this challenge are describing the Atlantic world context in which Aichison and Parker engaged distant markets as suppliers of forest products produced by slave labor in a unique extractive economy in the Lower Chesapeake. What are we to make of Aichison and Parker as enslavers who transported at least two enslaved people for sale in distant Atlantic ports? Given the thin records regarding Aichison and Parker's Atlantic business, what might we learn from the records of other local outfits, including Dismal Plantation, a slave labor camp located in the swamp between 1765 and the early 1780s? What might the records that reference the plantation's key overseers—John Augustine Washington, Jacob Collee, and John Driver—reveal about the people forced to labor in the swamp? And how did the broader swamp change over time as local outfits sought to claim space in it during the earliest years of the republic?

Though the Great Dismal Swamp remained a largely underdeveloped backwater of the Lower Chesapeake at the time of the American war for independence, Virginia and North Carolina speculators turned their attentions to the area during ensuing two decades. These speculators used enslaved labor to build on the infrastructure and institutions established by the previous generation. Working in the extreme spring and summer heat and humidity, enslaved shinglers established timber camps and constructed roads, while enslaved canal laborers dug waterways small and large that facilitated trade in the Lower Chesapeake region's primary industry, the production of timber shingles and staves, and in the secondary industries involving naval stores such as tar, pitch, and turpentine.[8]

Prior to 1815, forest products and naval stores drove a regional extractive economy that fed local agricultural and retail trades that serviced Atlantic markets near and far.[9] To explain the first period of this story of change in the 1780s and 1790s, this chapter primarily centers on the questions raised in an examination of correspondence between two Dismal Swamp Company (DSC) men—company shareholder David Jameson and company agent John

Driver. We can tease out of this business correspondence the earliest years in which petit marronage undergirded the DSC's operations.

By 1700, the Virginia colony was settled in distinct regions: the tidewater in the east, the mountainous ridges and valleys of the west, and the piedmont in the center. Crossed by four deep, wide tidal rivers that generally coursed from west to east—the Potomac, the Rappahannock, the York, and the James—the Virginia tidewater centered along the southern half of the Chesapeake Bay. At the southern end of the bay, near its watershed into the Atlantic Ocean, the Lower Chesapeake region almost entirely comprised the Dismal Swamp. The region's central port town, Norfolk, was established in 1682 at the mouth of the Elizabeth River's eastern shore and by 1770 had a population of 3,000. Twenty miles southwest of Norfolk lay Suffolk, established in 1742 as a port on the Nansemond River, on the Great Dismal's northwestern fringe. On the western bank of the Elizabeth, across from Norfolk, lay Portsmouth, a secondary port established in 1752. At more than 440,000, Virginia had the highest population among the British North American colonies by 1770. More than 40 percent of this population were enslaved people.

North Carolina was chartered as an English proprietary colony in the mid-1660s, with areas of settlement subsequently taking root in the Lower Cape Fear River Valley near Wilmington, at the head of the Pamlico Sound at New Bern, and across the piedmont and westward into the Blue Ridge Mountains, an area known as the backcountry by the turn of the century. By the late 1720s, when the colony reverted to British Crown control, the colony's distinct regional geographic districts included Albemarle, Bath, Granville, the Upper and Lower Cape Fear areas, the backcountry, and the piedmont. In the Albemarle district, settlements were established at Bath on the Pamlico River in 1705 and at Edenton at the mouth of the Chowan River in 1722. Edenton became the colonial capital, in part as a result of the location's proximity to the Chesapeake Bay to the north.[10] The Great Dismal Swamp region remained largely rural even as the colony's population grew to nearly two hundred thousand by 1770, fifth-highest among the British North American colonies.

As British colonial merchants in Norfolk and Portsmouth prior to the American Revolution, Aichison and Parker viewed the swamp not as a refuge but as an opportunity. The two men were situated at one point of an Atlantic world network of trade that depended on access to the Dismal's most precious resources—its old-growth cypress, juniper, and pine trees. Aichison and Parker, in turn, connected those products to far-flung markets in Cuba, the Canaries, and beyond. Within two years of the creation of the Aichison and Parker firm in 1758, it employed Thomas Macknight to build and operate a store in Winfield, a hamlet located on the Pasquotank River in North Carolina's Albemarle district. To support this venture, Aichison and Parker financed Thomas Macknight and Company, a firm that gave them access to the colony's wheat, pork, pine tar, lumber, and retail trades. Macknight acquired land patents and purchased property on which he sought to build roads, providing his benefactors in Norfolk with better access. Products manufactured in North Carolina flowed north, influencing the growth of Suffolk, a town with a public wharf suitable for small vessels in the West Indies trade.[11]

Aichison and Parker's ledger provides evidence of an important resourcefulness on the part of people who have long captured literary and scholarly interest. Though the document provides no further information about the Dismal's mysterious furniture maker, it does tell us that he not only had created his wares within the swamp but also had used the swamp for subsistence. Most important, the ledger shows that the furniture maker remained connected to the world outside the swamp through the wares he produced. Thus, Aichison and Parker sought to transform the landscape that supported the furniture maker's refuge.

Aichison and Parker likely included the anecdote about the black swamper as a matter of passing interest: to them, the novelty of his tale of thirteen years in the swamp reflected more hyperbole than truth. As their firm began constructing the Dismal's infrastructure, however, they and other land speculators chafed at the notion of a wilderness claimed by people living on the margins, outside of Virginia's social and political hierarchies. Schemes to improve the Dismal's swampscape and ultimately to bring local people into closer accord with colonial officials were proposed as early as 1728, when Virginia governor William Byrd II toured the swamp. The first effort to drain the swamp occurred in May 1762, when former Norfolk County mayor Robert Tucker claimed one thousand acres on the Dismal's eastern fringe and dispatched an enslaved crew to begin the construction of a causeway. In March 1763, the plans to drain the swamp to create arable lands were made public.[12]

Historical marker commemorating the site where enslaved people dug the first canal to Lake Drummond. The 4.5 mile stretch was chosen in 1763, after George Washington's swamp survey. Photo by the author.

Two months later, on May 25, 1763, the DSC announced its incorporation. Its shareholders included Tucker; William and Thomas Nelson, father and son planters from Yorktown; Dr. Thomas Walker; George Washington; Washington's brother-in-law, Fielding Lewis; John Robinson; Robert Burwell; William Waters; John Syme; Anthony Bacon; and Samuel Gist. Soon thereafter, Washington, Lewis, and two others toured the swamp's fringes on horseback, finding sandy soils unsuitable for agriculture. But having observed the swamp's Green Sea—open lands and tall reeds in the northwestern part of the swamp—Washington became convinced that the inner swamp's black soils were fertile. Rendering this landscape arable would constitute a major project involving managers to establish land claims with county surveyors, the production or purchase of a variety of tools, the purchase of land near the swamp to serve as a base of operations, and most important, the purchase of enslaved people who would be compelled to perform the arduous labor of cutting paths and irrigation ditches, clearing a camp, planting and tending to crops, and maintaining the DSC's property.

To bring this project to fruition, DSC officials established Dismal Town on a 402-acre tract of land six miles south of Suffolk and centered in a swamp field known as White Marsh. DSC officials rented the property from Mills Riddick, who owned the largest plantation in the Virginia Southside in Nansemond County. Washington temporarily resided at Dismal Plantation, but the DSC's managers named Washington's younger brother, John Augustine Washington, the plantation's resident overseer. By July 1763, John Augustine Washington managed the labors of fifty-four enslaved people: forty-three men, nine women, one boy, and one girl. The enslaved laborers cleared a sector of old cypress and cedar trees and younger red and white oaks, maples, and elms and dug an irrigation ditch three feet deep and ten feet wide. The ditch extended five miles from Dismal Plantation to Lake Drummond and was intended to bring water into the lake to create arable land. The enslaved laborers also shaved the oldest white cedar trees into more than ten thousand eighteen-inch shingles, which became the extracted natural resources that provided the earliest of the DSC's profits.

In January 1764, the DSC signaled its deepening commitments to Dismal Plantation and to the use of slave labor when it secured the backing of both the Virginia House of Burgesses and the Commonwealth Council in the form of a law that granted the company the right to dig canals or to build causeways through land adjacent to the Dismal. Anticipating later suits, the law protected the company against claims for damages entered in county courts on the grounds that the company's projects would benefit the public good. The following December, the DSC partners met in Williamsburg and purchased one thousand acres in Nansemond County adjoining the road connecting Suffolk to Norfolk. For this tract of land, the partners envisioned enslaved laborers cutting a canal to connect the company's holdings to the Nansemond River.[13] At the Williamsburg meeting, the shareholders also discussed their concerns regarding the flight of enslaved laborers at Dismal Plantation. Aiming to bolster the labor force and believing that increasing the number of women would reduce their male counterparts' propensity to engage in petit marronage, the partners voted that each would send four more enslaved men and one enslaved woman to Dismal Plantation.[14]

By early 1765, therefore, the DSC shareholders had pledged to send to Dismal Plantation as many as forty-eight more enslaved men and twelve more women, in an effort to curtail slave flight. Nevertheless, enslaved men continued to "run about" Nansemond County at night. Virginia's first newspaper, the *Virginia Gazette*, published notices for more than thirty-five hundred runaways between 1736 and 1783. In June 1768, John Augustine Washington in-

Historical marker commemorating the site where the Dismal Swamp Land Company established Dismal Town in 1763. Photo by the author.

formed readers that "a new negro man named Tom" had fled "the proprietors of the Dismal Swamp" in April 1767. Tom stood about five feet, six inches tall and bore "his country marks," four on each cheek. Washington offered a reward of three pounds sterling for Tom's return. In October 1768, John Mayo, soon to sit in the Virginia House of Burgesses and later a delegate to the 1775 convention, placed another ad seeking Tom. Mayo described the runaway as "about 6 feet high," with a "roguish look"; he also had "lost part of one of his ears." Tom had been seen "in Nansemond and Norfolk counties" but "is supposed to be about the Dismal Swamp." In April 1769, the Virginia Gazette ran a third advertisement for Tom, again describing him as approximately six feet tall with one cropped ear. However, Mayo added that he now believed Tom to be "about the Dismal Swamp. or low down in North-Carolina." Mayo also raised the reward for Tom's capture to ten pounds.[15]

As archaeologist Daniel Sayers has observed, John Augustine Washington's and Mayo's advertisements confirm that people were marooned in the Great Dismal Swamp but nevertheless fail to provide further information that would assist in scholarly efforts to clearly define such instances as either short-term (petit) or long-term (grand) marronage.[16] Whatever the extent of Tom's movements about the swamp, Tom's case unquestionably constitutes petit marronage. Furthermore, the increases in the reward for Tom's return testify to the growing value Washington and Mayo placed on recapturing him as the DSC's commitment to slavery deepened and as both his time in flight and potential distance from Dismal Plantation increased.

As Tom fled and the DSC sought to claim space in the Dismal by expanding its operations, Aichison, Parker, and Macknight stood to profit from the improved infrastructure. In 1761, Macknight sought a land patent of fourteen hundred acres on the swamp's southern edge from the Granville proprietary. Not long after Aichison, Parker, and Macknight received word of the DSC's formation, the three men conceived a plan to form another business venture, the Campania Company, that would carry out their existing plan to drain land in the North Carolina sector of the swamp as well as incorporate their claim to protect it against DSC claims in North Carolina. On March 26, 1763, Macknight entered a patent of seven hundred acres, while Samuel Johnston, recently appointed as clerk of the North Carolina Superior Court, entered a patent of twenty-eight acres. Three weeks later, Macknight entered another patent of fifty-six hundred acres. The Campania Company's land claims lay unimproved for the remainder of the decade, however, and in February 1770, the DSC secured a land patent that encompassed forty thousand acres, including all Dismal swampland in North Carolina.[17]

During the American War for Independence of the 1770s and early 1780s, the company's partners did not regularly meet, no doubt because some, including George Washington, were directly engaged in the war effort. Extant company records offer limited information about events at Dismal Plantation during these years, and the advertisements seeking Tom's return seem to suggest a limited scope for marronage. However, engaging the DSC's records in new ways seems to indicate that Dismal Plantation's enslaved people essentially became marooned in the swamp under limited oversight. The plantation fell into significant disrepair during the war, and operations subsequently did not restart easily, with slave flight remaining a problem. In 1784, English traveler J. F. D. Smyth published *A Tour in the United States of America*, an account of his travels through the new country intended for British audiences. According to Smyth, it was common knowledge among Virginians that enslaved runaways found refuge in the

Great Dismal, residing there for "twelve, twenty, or thirty years and upwards" and subsisting on "corn, hogs, and fowls" they raised "on some of the spots not perpetually under water, nor subject to be flooded, as forty-nine out of fifty parts of it are." In addition, the maroons "have erected habitations, and cleared small fields around them." These clearings were located in swamp sectors that had "always been perfectly impenetrable to any of the inhabitants of the country around."[18]

Smyth's account of Virginians' knowledge of the Dismal's maroons could well have been the stories of distinct maroon camps. His accounts could also have been based on stories told by those who knew of Dismal Plantation or of several other camps of enslaved shinglers and canal cutters established by the early 1780s. Smyth's omission of the sources of his information constitutes another form of archival silence, but further evidence of the contours of Dismal Plantation can be gleaned from extant DSC records. On December 5, 1783, David Jameson, a minor shareholder who lived in York, penned a letter to John Driver, the company's agent in Suffolk, that reveals key details regarding the DSC's attempts to revive its postwar operations by establishing a market in Antigua. Several years earlier, Driver's father, also his predecessor as the company's agent, had died without having properly settled up with the DSC, leaving the company on the hook for his expenses. Since Driver was also the executor of his father's estate, Jameson asked him to provide any relevant information regarding the elder Driver's account "and do what is necessary in that business."[19] Driver thus found himself at the intersection of competing interests: the company for which he now acted as agent was indebted to his father's estate, for which he was executor.

Jameson's letter brought up another matter of interest as well: what to do with "an outlying fellow belonging to the D.S.Co. called Tom." According to shareholder David Meade, Tom needed "to be sold," and Jameson agreed, directing Driver arrange the sale, which Jameson hoped would bring "seventy or eighty pounds."[20] If this was the same Tom who had slipped away from Dismal Plantation in 1767, the DSC apparently had apprehended him in late 1783, after he had spent more than sixteen years marooned in the Dismal. But extant records contain no further mentions of Tom or of his sale, which means he might have remained in the swamp's inner depths.

A letter written by Driver in 1790 reveals that in 1775, Jacob Collee, the company's agent at Suffolk, had overseen enslaved laborers at Dismal Plantation, "most of them Fellows & at least 40 good working hands with Tools of every kind" necessary for the efficient operation of the plantation. Collee also oversaw nearly thirty head of cattle and a few sheep and hogs.[21] Driver did not explain the transition in oversight from John Augustine Washington to Collee or the significant drop in the number of enslaved people at Dismal Plantation. In what would become a normal pattern of correspondence, the letters that passed among Driver, Jameson, and other DSC officials reflect their key concerns, which included shingles, provisions for Dismal Plantation, and the full proceeds from a cask of rice in Antigua, all of which received more attention than the proposal to sell Tom.

Other letters reveal additional reasons that Dismal Plantation foundered. Writing in June 1783 from Castle Hill in Albemarle County, Thomas Walker delegated to Jameson and other DSC officials authority to set the price of the rice produced at Dismal Plantation and set aside the question of whether the company would hire more enslaved laborers to be sent into the swamp until officials could meet in person. The most important business involved the effort to secure by land survey the DSC's claim in the swamp.[22] Several days later, Walker wrote again, adding important details to the problem of the land survey and cost. Because the company had paid its taxes, to deny any part of the claim would comprise the highest form of "injustice" assuming that the original forty-thousand-acre tract remained legally vacant. But to think that such a tract of valuable land remained free of squatters, competing land speculators, or enslaved people engaged in marronage was folly. Walker thus offered Jameson a keen bit of advice: if any person were to occupy the land illegally, he should mobilize the DSC's lawyers to prosecute the intruder or to return him or her to an enslaver.[23]

By October 1783, DSC agent Robert Andrews had overseen the completion of the Dismal Swamp survey; nevertheless, Jameson believed, "many disputes are likely to arise as our title to all or indeed to any part" of the swamp, since the DSC's claim was subject to contest in court by others who had also surveyed land tracts.[24] Consequently, Jameson suggested strongly that the DSC shareholders meet the following month to plan carefully its next steps. That meeting did not occur, and in late December, Andrews reported that the Nansemond County surveyor had not yet validated Andrews's survey with a signature. The plat for the DSC's claim would not be ready by Jameson's next visit to York.[25]

In the spring of 1784, Jameson penned a particularly long letter in which he countered Meade's assertion that the company was bankrupt. According to Jameson, "we have been taught by our Country that Funds and Money are two different things." During the "age of paper," Jameson had deposited receipts in the loan office, and he currently held 12,000 pounds sterling in paper certificates. Since the "*Golden Age*" had returned, he had collected 100 pounds from Collee and had written the DSC secretary to recover nearly 150 pounds spent on the "hire of a negro," though the secretary apparently had no money. Jameson had also delegated to William Nelson the effort to collect on Thomas Walker's bond but did not expect payment in time to suit the DSC's present concerns. Even Byrd, who had carried Meade's letter to York, was in debt to the company, which also had outstanding debts for "Rice sold last year." Jameson seemed to be working to collect enough money to pay Andrews to secure the land claim in the Dismal, and he lamented the fact that the company had not yet held a meeting in Richmond to coordinate all of these efforts. If a meeting had taken place, the company might have prioritized the land claim or extended it to cover the whole of the swamp, "agreeable to the original orders of Council." A subcommittee had decided that the company should go to court to pursue a claim for the entire swamp, leading Jameson to return the survey of the forty thousand acres and plat to the land registry office.[26]

The partners' first postwar meeting came in Richmond in early May 1785. During the first day, the partners discussed raising the money to pay for a survey of the forty thousand acres and subdividing the tract proportionally according to the number of quarter shares each partner held and voted to bring Collee before the partners to settle his accounts before permitting him to leave the company's service. On the second day, the partners approved a motion to hire white laborers from Baltimore or to hire enslaved laborers until the company could find up to three hundred Dutch or German immigrant laborers with knowledge of ditch agriculture. Before the meeting closed, the partners considered several more pressing matters: strangers' encroachments on company land; authorization to purchase adjacent tracts or extant mills; and the withdrawals of and replacements for Walker and George Washington from active participation in the company's affairs.[27]

The proposal to consider other sources of labor represented a key shift from the exclusive use of enslaved people held by the original partners to a labor force comprised of slaves hired from local slaveholders or purchased at local slave auctions. With slavery's future in the new United States in question, the partners may have considered the change in operations as others among Virginia's elites considered private manumissions or gradual emancipation. Alternatively, the new approach may have reflected Jameson and the other partners' acknowledgment that ten years of efforts to exploit slave labor to carve a plantation out of the swamp's cedar trees had little changed the landscape. The partners replaced Collee with John Driver.

In December 1784, Collee had sent an enslaved laborer to Jameson with a letter requesting instructions regarding the plantation's annual management. Jameson then wrote to William Nelson to recommend that the DSC shareholders hire "*at least* ten strong hands for the year." If the shareholders approved the proposal, Jameson would direct Collee to "hire ten able hands." But because Jameson was unsure that the company could afford to buy additional laborers, Jameson advised Collee to "hire what hands he thought *really necessary to work the Crop.*"[28] By the summer of 1785, with Driver now overseeing operations, the DSC resumed production of shingles at Dismal Plantation using not white indentured laborers from Baltimore or recently arrived laborers from the Netherlands or Germany but enslaved people. While Jameson held out hope that the company might still import a significant group of European laborers, Driver focused on the problems the plantation now presented, particularly the disrepair that plagued the plantation's irrigation and drainage ditches. In the fall of 1785, with Driver in Suffolk, Jameson and Nathaniel Nelson, another son of William Nelson, took the lead of overseeing the plantation's affairs on behalf of the partners.[29]

By August 1786, Driver began to submit regular reports of his observations of Dismal Plantation. Although Driver believed that a new swamp land tract might yield a profit in shingles, the current plantation needed repairs, and he requested that the company send someone to advise him not only about how to proceed but also how to manage the enslaved laborers who had been there for at least a decade. The "Remnant of old Negroes there is by no means sufficient to keep the place in order," Driver wrote, "the Ditches are much broke & require a deal of work on them, the present Crop is almost downed there will be but little Corn made."[30] It is unclear exactly who this "remnant" was—the men and women sent into the swamp in the 1760s, those mentioned in the plantation's accounts in 1775, or both. But there is no question that Driver was becoming increasingly unhappy with their labors and with the shareholders' reluctance to send even more enslaved people. At the beginning of 1787, Jameson told Driver that the company was having difficulty purchasing new enslaved laborers, in part because of lack of capital but also because "no person inclines to hire their Negroes to work at the Swamp." Jameson instead proposed using "white servants," who might arrive by the spring. Demonstrating the significance of these problems, Jameson reported that William Nelson intended to visit the swamp to provide recommendations regarding the plantation's improvement.[31]

In late February 1787, Driver advised Jameson that in the absence of additional enslaved laborers, Dismal Plantation was no longer worth maintain-

ing. The "present set of hands" had only "made Corn for to serve the Plantation," and the previous "wet season" had rendered the plantation's crop of
rice and shingles unprofitable. Driver had purchased clothing and pork to
sustain the plantation's inhabitants and intended to acquire fish for the same
purpose.[32] By June, Driver's outlook brightened. Despite the struggles of
the previous year, Driver anticipated a "pretty good Crop of Corn and Rice"
if the weather and "the hands" cooperated.[33] By October, however, Driver's
optimism had waned: although about forty thousand shingles were on hand,
the "dryness of the Summer" meant that the rice crop would again fail. Further, Driver explained, the plantation and ditches were "much out of order,"
and with only the "Remnant of worn out Negroes" at the plantation, ditch
repairs were all but impossible.[34]

In February 1788, Driver reported to Jameson that about three thousand
barrels of rice had been harvested and promised to send a barrel to York at
the next opportunity. However, Driver did not yet know how much the remaining crop would command, and the corn crop would again only suffice to provision the plantation. And perhaps most critically, the plantation's
profits would not cover its taxes, so Jameson would need to find money to
cover them.[35] In May 1788, Driver wrote again, again pleading with Jameson
for money to pay the taxes: "The Sheriff is now pursuing in his demands,"
Driver explained, and "the whole Tax is about £111," while not more than
"£20 or £30" was on hand.[36] Jameson then sent directions, and Driver accordingly received from the DSC treasurer forty pounds, fifteen shillings, and
nine pence, enabling the discharge of "so much of the Dismal Swamp Taxes
for the year 1786" but failing to satisfy the sheriff's lien for 1787.[37]

In June 1788, Driver sent more bad news: a small and low-quality rice
crop and ditches still in disrepair. The DSC had not supplied Driver with the
slaves he had sought, and those he did have lacked adequate provisions as
there was "hardly a Hogg on the Plantation." Driver consequently purchased
several sows and sent them to the plantation in hopes that they would repro-
duce and create a sustaining population that could feed the laborers.[38] Dismal Plantation's prospects improved little through the end of 1788. In early
1789, Driver reported that he would send along a barrel of rice to Jameson
but expressed surprise that company officials had not paid "more attention to
the place." And Driver painted a more dire picture of the situation on Dismal Plantation: "It is impossible for the present number of hands to do any
thing tolerable," he lamented, and "the Ditches all want repairing & require
a great deal of labour to do it." On the plus side, he noted, the plantation
had produced one hundred thousand shingles, for which Driver now had to

find a market.[39] In June, Driver reported that the rice crop and shingles were ready for market but that neither could be sold. The shingles fetched just under eight pounds per thousand on the local market, payable only in "Goods at the common retail prices." While the price for rice was higher, it, too, was payable only in local goods.[40]

The challenges of managing Dismal Plantation had taken their toll on Driver, and in June 1789, he told Jameson, "If you think the owners of the Swamp do not intend to put any more hands there, I wou'd wish to have nothing more to do with it." The plantation's deterioration was continuing, as were the sheriff's attempts to collect a "heavy Tax." Previous efforts to rectify Dismal Plantation's affairs had not borne fruit, despite Driver's strategy of deputizing one of the older enslaved people, Dempsey Smith, as "foreman," overseeing daily operations while Driver relocated to Suffolk, visiting the plantation two or three times a week.[41] Driver was also looking for other lands for the company to purchase as sites for new sawmills that could more efficiently carve timber into shingles. Driver had personally purchased a six-acre-tract at Jericho Mill Stream, several miles south of Suffolk on the road to Norfolk, for 109 pounds. The property included an old dam that needed repair and sufficient timber for both a mill and building gates to control the stream's flow. And Driver intended to sell the property to the DSC.[42]

In July, Driver indicated that he intended to charge just under thirteen pounds per thousand for the crop of shingles produced by enslaved people at Dismal Plantation. Noting that it was a "busy time in the Crop," Driver requested confirmation from Jameson that the shingles would find a market and permission to hire cartage for them.[43] The following month, Driver reported that forty-six thousand shingles were "subject to a great loss": sixteen thousand lay waiting for a vessel to carry them from Suffolk to Yorktown, while the remainder, worth as much as seventy pounds per thousand, awaited a market. Driver requested an update on officials' decision regarding the mill he had recently acquired, pointing out that he had purchased and improved it for the company's benefit. Driver now had "very serious intentions of removing to the Western Country" within the coming twelve months, and if the company was not interested in buying the mill, the man from whom Driver had purchased it "has offer'd me other property that will suit me better."[44]

In early September 1789, Driver apologized to Jameson for yet another crop of poor shingles unsuitable for any "good buildings," though they had passed inspection at Suffolk as "far better than one half that are bought to this market." With Smith overseeing the plantation, the enslaved shingle getters had cut poorer quality shingles than Driver had anticipated, perhaps in a subtle act of resistance. As a result, Driver advised Jameson to continue the search for an able overseer. The operation had yielded fifty thousand shingles, a slight increase from the number reported earlier in the summer, and they continued to sell for just under eight pounds per thousand in Suffolk.[45]

Later in the month, Driver again wrote to Jameson, conveying the news that shingles that had recently found buyers should be ready by the end of October and that tree bark might be purchased at fifteen pounds per thousand as a consequence of the lack of a full crew of enslaved laborers at Dismal Plantation. He continued to hope that the DSC "wou'd send more hands to the swamp that something might be made that wou'd better inable them" to cut shingles more quickly and in greater numbers. But the prospect of getting better shingles to market had not improved, and Driver recognized that the DSC might censure him if he continued producing low-quality shingles. Driver complained that Jameson and the DSC were "unacquainted with the difficulties in making anything there with a few old worn out Negroes" and noted that William Nelson had "discharged from service in 1785" four of the plantation's enslaved laborers "as incapable of labour for which they really are." Nevertheless, they were still "supported with Provision," making them essentially "an intire Tax" on the plantation's operations. Though Collee, who had "work'd the Plantation as long as cou'd be done without ever touching a Ditch," might have responded to the plantation's enslaved laborers' lack of activity with tacit acceptance, Driver had spent more than two years directing the enslaved laborers to repair the ditches, to little effect.[46]

By December 1789, the DSC's shingling operations at Dismal Plantation appeared to be on sounder footing. Driver had 50,000 shingles on hand for one account and had arranged for 150,000 more eighteen-inch shingles to be ready for market in the West Indies by mid-January, when Harrison Allmand was prepared to purchase them for nearly eight pounds per thousand. Driver advised Jameson to accept Allmand's offer, which would save the DSC the expense of carting them as well prevent them from rotting and thus depreciating.[47] In mid-January, however, the vessel Driver had expected to ferry the shingles had not arrived, and "every Craft here is employed in the Norfolk business & will not take a freight to York on any Terms."[48]

At the beginning of May, Driver penned another letter offering keen insight into the reasons that shingle production at Dismal Plantation continued to struggle. The plantation's enslaved crew had not cut any boards in the swamp except what they "get in their own time on Sundays & Nights." The rest of their time was spent tending to the plantation's rice, corn, hogs, and other provision crops. Though the shingles were "better than common" and though they might sell for ten pounds per thousand, carting them to Suffolk would pose a problem, since the plantation's enslaved carters, too, were "busy in the Crop."[49] As Driver had for years explained to company officials, the enslaved crew was simply not large enough to perform all the labor needed to produce crops for sale, produce provisions, and maintain the irrigation ditches. In addition, the company's main concern was shingles, yet the endowed laborers' primary efforts were devoted to other areas. Under these circumstances, the number of shingles the company sourced would remain small, and the DSC's efforts to claim additional ground in the swamp would be hindered. Driver's letter also offers insight into the plantation's enslaved crew. It is reasonable to assume that the shinglers resisted being overworked and that the plantation's agents and overseers—Collee, Driver, and Smith—had not been able to extract further labor from them either by force or by negotiation.

In early August 1790, Driver announced that the "hands are employed at the swamp in getting the shingles." Setting the price for the shingles at sixteen pounds per thousand, Driver explained that not all of the current yield would be comprised of "heart" planks, but they would be of a "good thickness" and would include "such sap ones" as the old timber the company's enslaved shinglers were currently cutting. Driver anticipated that, by the middle of September, the forced laborers he oversaw might produce fifty thousand shingles.[50] But early in the next shingling season, the problems had recurred, with Driver writing in February 1791 that no shingles were available at the swamp and that the "Overseer at the Swamp tells me that it will not be possible to get any until next Fall." Yet again, according to Driver, the plantation was "so out of Order for want of the Ditches being opened & a quantity of new Fencing made" that no shingling could occur until those repairs were undertaken.[51]

From the mid-1760s to the early 1790s, Dismal Plantation remained a haphazard operation, and extant records show little change in the observations made by company officials. And these documents also show that agents and overseers could do little to compel enslaved laborers to perform even routine maintenance tasks or to prevent slaves from fleeing. Tom, who fled John Augustine Washington in 1767, remained on the run for nearly twenty years. Driver's letters reveal continued dissatisfaction with the enslaved people at Dismal Plantation, who evidently resisted his demands. By late 1789, Dismal Plantation was essentially a maroon camp under the most limited of indirect oversight by company agents based at Suffolk.

The DSC was not alone in claiming space in the swamp. As early as January 1790, Robert Andrews had explained "no effectual stop can possibly be put to the encroachments made on the Company's Land" without regular prosecution and legal claims to recover damages from competing land speculators.[52] In July 1791, Driver wrote to Jameson that two men, Isaac Sexton and John Cowper, had been "getting large Quantity of Timber of the Land suppos'd to belong to the Dismal Swamp" company. Sexton owned several acres of dry land near the swamp at Deep Creek, Virginia, and had constructed a road into the swamp, where "hands imployed by Mr. Cowper & himself . . . get a very considerable quantity" of shingles. Driver had informed Sexton that he and Cowper were not permitted to cut shingles on DSC land claims, but the two men had made it clear that they intended to continue their operation.[53]

Driver offered Jameson shrewd advice that reveals not only the value local land speculators placed on Dismal Swamp shingles but also the fact that the DSC was not the only show in town. Driver's advice also reveals the fact that the DSC and other land speculators needed slave labor to realize their envisioned profits. According to Driver, if Sexton agreed to pay the DSC the value of the timber his men cut, "I think it wou'd be well to let him have it."[54] Not only would doing so avoid the expense of fighting the incursion in court, the company would obtain some income without going to the trouble of finding a crew of slave laborers and attempting to induce them to labor under the oppressive conditions of swamp work.

CHAPTER 2

"Lawless Sette of Villains"

Petit Marronage and the Competition for Space in the Turn-of-the-Century Swamp

During the American Revolution, the movements of fugitive slaves and maroons to the lines of British forces, colonial militias, and Continental troops exacerbated fears regarding uncontrolled slaves, and these fears persisted after the peace of 1783. Slave flight in North Carolina increased in the 1790s, with an uptick in private manumissions by Quakers, who took their cues from broader antislavery trends in the Atlantic world. Readers of Atlantic world correspondence in the Lower Chesapeake also observed closely the Haitian Revolution in the former French colony of Saint-Domingue, fearing a similar uprising closer to home.[1] In June and July 1795, the *Wilmington Gazette* observed that a band of enslaved runaways "in the daytime secrete[d] themselves in the swamps and woods and at night committed various depredations on the neighbouring plantations" in the Lower Cape Fear River Valley of North Carolina. After the militia dislodged the runaways from the swamp where they had found refuge, local officials learned that the group had been led by one "who styled himself The General of the Swamps." The band had killed at least one white man and was accused of severely wounding another. By mid-July, the local militia had responded by killing nine of the maroons, including the leader, but a new leader emerged and several runaways were still on the lam.[2]

These events suggest the primary reason why white Virginians and North Carolinians might fear a runaway group engaged in petit marronage: if they remained in flight, such groups might perpetuate their existence by organizing to defend the space they claimed. The Wilmington maroons' resistance found its mirror in Jamaica's Second Maroon War, an eight-month guerrilla action waged by Trelawny Town against British troops that began in August 1795. During the war, the Windward Maroons of Charles, Moore, and Scott's Hall Towns remained neutral, while the maroons of Accompong Town sided with the British forces. In December 1795, facing defeat at the hands of maroon forces outnumbered ten to one, General George Walpole and colonial governor Alexander Lindsay, Earl of Balcarres, initiated a campaign intended to isolate the Trelawny Town maroons from vital subsistence provisions and to destroy maroon farms and supplies. The Trelawny Town maroons capitulated on the condition that they would not be deported; Walpole required the Trelawny maroons to kneel and beg for the British king's forgiveness, to return enslaved people who had fled local plantations to join the maroons' ranks, and to relocate to another part of the island. The Trelawny maroons nevertheless continued to engage British troops until March 1796, and Lindsay argued that the maroons had breached the terms of their capitulation before he ordered their deportation to Nova Scotia. After several difficult years there, the Trelawny Town maroons relocated to the British West African colony of Sierra Leone.[3]

While archival silences hinder further knowledge of Wilmington's swamp general and the maroon group that he led, reports of the presence of a swamp general suggest the degree to which the group had organized. The group was more than a mere runaway band: it had become a maroon community. That phenomenon alone provided the area's white population with a motivation for reining in maroon groups. And instances of marronage were not limited to the forests and swamps near Wilmington. In an advertisement published on March 2, 1793, Whitmill Hill warned readers of the paper published in Edenton, the *State Gazette of North Carolina*, that an escaped slave, Yarmouth, "may be lurking about Edenton." Later that month, Stephen Cabarrus posted an advertisement for Isaac, citing "reasons to believe that he is lurking in Perquimans County," where he had recently married a woman.[4] In an advertisement published on March 23 in the New Bern paper, the *North-Carolina Gazette, or Impartial Intelligencer and Weekly Advertizer*, Edward Witty of Jones County similarly informed readers that "a Negro fellow named NED alias DICK" had absconded about a month earlier. Witty speculated that Ned was "lurking about in the neighbourhood, or [had] gone with Mr. Pollock's Negroes, towards Edenton." In a statement that suggested Witty's intent to close all of Ned's avenues for escaping North Carolina, Witty offered a reward of three pounds for Ned's return and warned all masters of vessels in Edenton against "harbouring him" or transporting him out of the state.[5]

The locations mentioned in these advertisements are noteworthy. The possibility that Ned had remained in Jones County indicates the existence of petit marronage in the northernmost reaches of the Upper Cape Fear River in southeastern North Carolina. But Witty also had reason to believe that Ned had sought to reach Edenton, a port town with almost sixteen hundred residents on the Albemarle Sound in Chowan County, and both it and Perquimans County had more Great Dismal swampland than improved farmland. If Ned had indeed sought to make his way more than 120 miles north, he would likely have traveled by water, perhaps along a clandestine route inside North Carolina's barrier islands. But Ned could also have followed the more difficult land routes once traveled by the Tuscarora and other Native American groups, through the Alligator Swamp along the south shore of Albemarle Sound. If so, he would have passed within a few miles of property owned by the Lake Company, which Josiah Collins and two business partners had established in 1786, the same year the North Carolina General Assembly banned slave importations from Africa. Through the Lake Company, Collins and his partners purchased eighty enslaved persons imported directly from West Africa aboard the *Camden*. Their labors to fell trees and to build navigable canals undergirded the Lake Company's efforts to transform its claim in Alligator Swamp into North Carolina's largest nineteenth-century plantation, Somerset Place.[6]

During these years, agents of the Dismal Swamp Company (DSC) complained not of maroons but of local outfits such as the Bear Quarter Company, a "lawless sette of villains" engaged in cutting timber in the DSC's swamp tracts. Company agents nevertheless remained apprehensive regarding petit marronage. Fears of slave rebellion loomed, particularly because enslaved watermen and enslaved women and children moved about either with passes or clandestinely. What, then, can we learn about the DSC and other outfits that claimed space in the swamp from the records of the region's primary land and canal companies—the DSC and the Dismal Swamp Canal Company? What can we learn about petit marronage and informal slave economies of exchange? How might the answers to these questions inform our understanding of white Virginians' and North Carolinians' fears regarding enslaved blacks in flight?

Yarmouth, Isaac, and Ned reflect the broader population of absconders engaged in petit marronage. These freedom's seekers, alongside Tom, who absconded from Dismal Plantation in 1767, and the Dismal's black furniture maker, posed perhaps the most complex problems for white Virginians and North Carolinians. But if these runaways reached the Great Dismal, they might discover the camps established by the DSC or its competitors where enslaved persons labored with minimal oversight. And these camps might accept absconders who could contribute to group subsistence in the swamp.

In their seminal work, *Runaway Slaves: Rebels on the Plantation*, John Hope Franklin and Loren Schweninger pointed to the central place that slave flight occupies in any study of American slavery, synthesizing the studies that defined the contours of slave flight and black resistance. Franklin and Schweninger's framing provided an important context for more sustained study of slave runaway advertisements that had been published in edited volumes by scholars including Freddie L. Parker and Latham Windley. Taken together, these studies generally found that in Virginia and North Carolina, the majority of men, women, and children who took flight did not escape to distant regions. From the Lower Chesapeake, the reach of the Underground Railroad was limited, as runaways sought refuge in nearby geographies.[7]

Historians Bradford Wood and Larry Tise have explained that the rise in slave flight in North Carolina in the 1790s led the General Assembly, comprised mainly of slaveholding planters, to outlaw private manumissions and to empower sheriffs in the Lower Chesapeake to pursue "lurkers" in the Great Dismal Swamp.[8] Maroons who engaged the Lower Chesapeake's geography of resistance were forced to sever all but the most limited of ties to Virginia and North Carolina slave societies.[9] That rogue companies established new slave labor camps and that enslaved people continued to agitate for freedom suggest perhaps the most salient reason for white Virginians' and North Carolinians' fears: the vastness of both states' eastern tidal coastlands provided ample cover for marronage. The Great Dismal Swamp stood front and center in the minds of prominent men and their agents in the Chesapeake.

The extractive economy of slavery that took shape in the Great Dismal after the 1780s is but one of several more widely studied contexts involving race and slavery in the Atlantic world: the large-scale seventeenth- and eighteenth-century Caribbean sugar plantations of Caribbean islands; the Chesapeake tobacco plantations that flourished during those years; the rice and indigo enterprises of the eighteenth-century lowcountry; and the nineteenth-century cotton and sugar enterprises of the Deep South and Lower Mississippi River Valley. Scholars have most often contextualized the Dismal's extractive economy in comparison with smaller agricultural enterprises during the Age of Revolutions, proto-industrial enterprises such as the iron furnaces of Appalachia, and urban contexts of slavery along the Atlantic coast or in nineteenth-century piedmont towns including Richmond. The company officials who sought to establish the Lower Chesapeake's extractive economy drew on local networks of enslavers who themselves sought local markets for enslaved people in the years following the American Revolution, as Virginia and North Carolina's economies became more diversified. The camps established by company slaves became bases for a wide range of forest products—particularly wooden shingles and cypress boards—sold in Atlantic markets near and far. New forms of internal economy—of exchange in subsistence goods—took shape within the swamp as the numbers of enslaved people in the Dismal's camps increased after 1800. The success of the Lower Chesapeake's land and canal companies required these slave labor camps, and sustaining the camps required internal economies of exchange between enslaved laborers and maroons. Company officials therefore found it necessary to ignore the swamp's informal networks of exchange.

Slave flight and petit marronage occurred against a backdrop of significant change generated in part by British provincials' calls for liberty and in part by enslaved peoples' flight to British lines in search of freedom during the war. With long histories of legal codes that affirmed and protected slavery, most of the northern state legislatures began the process of gradual emancipation in the years following the war. In 1777, the Vermont Constitution declared no legal protections for holding enslaved people as private property, though it encoded caveats by which men and women might be "bound by their own consent." By the 1790s, Massachusetts had joined with Vermont in ending slavery altogether, though blacks in both states did not readily find in freedom the equality that the U.S. Constitution's framers had so vigorously promoted in justifying revolt against the British Parliament and Crown.[10] In southern New England and the mid-Atlantic, state legislatures acted slowly to pass gradual emancipation statutes, as partisans vigorously countered calls for black freedom with claims of the primacy of legal protections for private property in slaves.[11] Further south still, the situation was quite different. Maryland and Virginia vigorously debated but ultimately did not pass gradual emancipation laws.[12] North Carolina, South Carolina, and Georgia banned even private manumissions.[13]

New communities of freed blacks took root throughout the early republic, and the largest population of free blacks initially took shape in Virginia, but no large-scale effort to end American slavery, led by lawmakers in state legislatures, emerged from the American Revolution or the subsequent effort in the late 1780s to draft and adopt a new federal constitution. In Virginia and in other southern states, particularly in the new states of the Cotton Kingdom, slave populations and slavery-based economies expanded considerably. While eighteenth-century company records do not permit a definitive count, an increasing number of enslaved Virginians and North Carolinians found themselves rented to the companies operating in the Dismal Swamp. Beginning in the 1790s, DSC records show an increase in the operations of small outfits. In mid-August 1798, DSC agent Thomas Shepherd wrote to his superiors from New Mill Creek in Norfolk County that he had recently "prevented a number of people from crossing" the company's line "to commit depredations" in a sector known as Bear Quarter. In addition, he had driven off a small group of men already extracting timber, but they had returned, and whatever timber they did not cut, they burned in an act of "defiance" against Shepherd and the DSC. Shepherd had refrained from further confrontations with the trespassers, taking the advice of friends who believed that such efforts would "certainly" result in his death. He believed that driving off the intruders would require the local sheriff to enforce the DSC's line. And after sending the company's overseer to meet the intruders' leader, Thomas Wallace, Shepherd concluded that an attempt to bring suit against Wallace and the other proprietors of the Bear Quarter Company for damages would prove useless. At the same time, Shepherd perceived such activities as threatening the DSC's existence by resulting in the loss of "all their best Timber in this quarter." Though Wallace and the other intruders might not be held accountable in court, Shepherd thought that Norfolk County deputy surveyor Henry Smith might be: Smith, a member of the trespassing group, had instigated its actions when he crossed the company's line despite Shepherd's warning.[14]

A month later, Shepherd wrote again, informing DSC officials that the "Lawless Sette of Villains in Bear Quarter" were continuing to work the timber. They believed that the DSC had no legal right to the land and that the company needed to resurvey its claim for accuracy.[15] Having received no response to these two letters, Shepherd wrote a November memorandum to company managers in which he emphasized the need to act quickly to remove the trespassers and to preserve the timber. Shepherd reported that the proprietors of the Bear Quarter Company included Wallace, Matt Evans, Willis Leek, John Bartee, and Israel Freeman and that they were currently selling timber from the tract by the thousand, a volume that would make it easy to prove their depredations. Shepherd also named some of the "workmen" employed by the company: Josiah Morgan, Thomas Hodges, Jesse Wallace, and Enock Daily. In addition, the company employed more than a dozen "Negroes, which makes twenty Hands at work."[16]

The Bear Quarter trespassers' introduction of sixteen black people into the Dismal created another slave labor camp and created a point of entry for more potential maroons in the swamp. It also offered maroons already in the swamp another avenue for procuring subsistence supplies via the Dismal's informal exchange economy. Moreover, the new arrivals increased the swamp's black population relative to the handful of whites who supervised the slave laborers, potentially causing issues related to control. Such concerns appear not to have consumed the attention of the DSC's officials, but they were alarmed by the fact that the Bear Quarter Company was a competitor in the local slave hire marketplace. Earlier in the year, DSC managers had instructed Shepherd to advance the company's shingling aims, but the directions had arrived "too late in the Spring to Obtain hands." Given the "low price of shingles," he had no other options for enslaved laborers. Through the summer of 1798, Shepherd had accomplished little more than holding "possession" of the DSC's claims not currently encroached upon by the Bear Quarter group.[17]

By early January 1799, Shepherd had received no instructions regarding the Bear Quarter incursions. With John Brown having recently been appointed to join the DSC's managers, Shepherd wrote again to outline the Bear Quarter problem, reiterating the consequences of inaction against the Bear Quarter trespassers and adding that the trespassers could now cut and produce one hundred thousand shingles per month. Even worse, the Bear Quarter Company had contracted with George Capron, a shareholder in the Dismal Swamp Canal Company, to float shingles down the canal. Capron was a major buyer of shingles who had also developed secondary markets among local buyers. As a result, the Bear Quarter was thriving and comprised a "prodigious destruction" that would exhaust the natural resource in "a very short time." And the DSC's hold on other parts of its claim was tenuous at best.[18]

In the spring and summer of 1799, Shepherd sent two more letters describing the mounting problems facing the DSC's shingle enterprise: the

Norfolk County sheriff had refused to execute writs against the Bear Quarter people that the DSC hoped would result in their dispersal, and Shepherd had met with little success in advancing the company's shingling operations. However, Shepherd reported, the DSC's efforts to enforce its land claim had "very much alarmed" the Bear Quarter people, and they consequently "have stoped working over the line."[19]

Such a minor victory counted for little relative to the larger state of the company's affairs in the swamp. Shepherd nevertheless seemed optimistic regarding the prospects for the 1800 shingling season. By January of that year, Shepherd had all but written off the land tract the Bear Quarter group occupied: the intruders continued to work the timber, and "from the number of hands" they employed, "the timber must be Exosted by the middle of the Ensuing summer."[20] A few weeks later, Shepherd outlined his understanding of the competing claims to Dismal Swamp territory. William White of Princess Anne County had a land patent for a three-thousand-acre tract that dated to 1784, though a surveyor found that two-thirds of White's claim was preempted by the DSC's claim, leaving him with only seven hundred acres. White nonetheless continued to press his claim and had announced his intention to accompany a surveyor on a visit to the line dividing his tract from the DSC's claim. In addition, the Bear Quarter Company had been joined by intruders into other sectors of the DSC claim, among them a tract located between New Mill Creek and Suffolk.[21]

Reviewing documents relating to White's claim, Shepherd found new information suggesting that the Bear Quarter Company's claim might have predated that of the DSC. While the DSC claim dated to the mid-1760s, when Dismal Plantation was established, the plat was dated October 20, 1784, after the plats held by the Bear Quarter group. White had also provided documents that showed a mistake in the survey of the original land tract, which covered almost 52,600 acres, including Lake Drummond, rather than the 40,000 acres contained in the DSC's claim. The nearly 25 percent overage had not been recorded in the plat filed in the land office.[22] With the company already struggling to retain possession of its original claim, the mistake could only compound the problem of establishing the DSC's presence in the full survey tract. Yet the DSC had even more pressing problems. If it were challenged to prove its claim to the larger land area in court and defeated, Shepherd mused, the DSC might also be found to have been working in the wrong sector and then would "have no timber in this part" of Norfolk County.[23]

In May 1800, Shepherd began to regularly write to Thomas Swepson, the customs collector who in 1797 had succeeded John Driver as the DSC's Suffolk agent.[24] On May 16, Shepherd wrote that "the business between Bear Quarter people & The Company could not be compromised," and Norfolk County surveyor Robert Butt had petitioned to work timber on the DSC's claim. Shepherd counseled Swepson to advise the DSC directors that contracting with Butt or his associates would not be in the company's best interest, "as they are the principle people that dispute the company Title." The Butt claim represented a new group "now making new Locations over the Company lines."[25]

In June, Shepherd reported an unfavorable situation in the Norfolk County swamp sector, as "a number of people" had found "their Lands cut of by the companys line." Regarding White's effort to push forward a resurvey of the DSC's original charter, Shepherd had apprised Butt of the earlier surveying errors and then had been accused of "wishing to Claim the Present boundary" as including more land than had been covered by the original charter, since "every tree which I have cut, were not be upon the Companys Land." Because Shepherd's shinglers had cut in disputed zones, the Bear Quarter people and others continued their intrusions at "a terrible rate."[26]

The following month, Swepson summarized his knowledge of Shepherd's discussions with Butt and detailing his own interactions with the Norfolk County surveyor. Butt had proposed that both the DSC and Bear Quarter Company land titles be submitted to attorneys for examination, agreeing that if the DSC's claim preceded the Bear Quarter Company's, the latter would end its operations. Although Swepson thought that these terms "appeared reasonable," he lacked the authority to enter into such an agreement with Butt or the Bear Quarter people, and he noted that the DSC managers in Richmond had not responded to similar proposals during the preceding winter.[27]

In August 1800, Shepherd provided another update. Shepherd had surveyed the company's claim along the main road from Cooper's Mill in Nansemond County to the line dividing the company's territory from Isaac Sexton's claim. The Sexton line extended "a great distance lower down" than the company's claim but not "quite as far back as Mr Butt makes it." Butt, however, remained confident in Henry Smith's survey and produced a plat showing a discrepancy of 520 pales in the original charter survey. Shepherd had not been able to have his examination of Butt's survey verified by one of the county's sworn surveyors because Butt insisted that Smith's survey was accurate. More significantly, Shepherd again admitted, "I have not as yet worked a tree upon the Companys Lands [and] have Totally worked upon other peoples property which is, an actual trespass." As a result, Shepherd had recently been served a writ for damages and had been forced to seek compromises with the various "intruders" in the DSC's claim. These compromises would require the support of the company's directors, who could confer to Shepherd the authority to enter into agreements as he saw fit. Shepherd thus requested instructions from company officials.[28]

William Nelson finally responded to Swepson's July letter in October, addressing—but not resolving—several key issues raised by Swepson and Shepherd and explaining that the delay had resulted from the managers' inability to convene to discuss company business, to review White's and Butt's claims, and to visit Bear Quarter to observe the company's survey lines. Nelson had not yet been able to examine all of the papers involved, some of which were in the hands of other directors, and he asked Swepson to inform Butt and White that the managers intended to travel to Bear Quarter.[29]

The managers met in Richmond in January 1801 and passed a number of resolutions, including two key motions. The first authorized any two company managers and trustees to approve agents' requests to cut new canals on company lands and to enter into contracts to float timber down the "great Canal" (eventually known as the Dismal Swamp Canal), on which enslaved laborers had been working since 1794. By allowing the most active managers to approve such projects, officials sought to facilitate Shepherd's and Swepson's efforts to manage the business of the swamp. The second measure authorized the employment of a surveyor to run the DSC's lines and committed the company to investigating Sexton and Smith's survey line as well as White's claim. The January meeting also took care of property purchases and a variety of financial matters as well as approved John Brown's resignation as a manager and the appointments of the Reverend John Bracken, George Tucker, and Corbin Griffin to the board.[30]

The managers met again in June and authorized Swepson to facilitate the construction of a shingle road from Jericho Stream into a nearby tract of timber and to cut a canal from Jericho to Lake Drummond, giving him the power to purchase lands and contract with "any persons" to accomplish these tasks. Swepson thus had "full authority" to make many of the decisions that had previously fallen under the managers purview.[31] A year later, Shepherd wrote to Griffin, one of the new managers, providing an update on the situation in the swamp. By July 1801, the company was being pressured to pay "extravagant prices for carting and getting or not get any labourers," and the Bear Quarter people had become even more firmly entrenched, though "they are some distance beyond where my people work" as a consequence of Shepherd's deliberate efforts to stay away from them.[32]

In the spring of 1800, the residents of Richmond watched as Federalists and Democratic Republicans vigorously competed for seats in the Virginia General Assembly. Among DSC and Dismal Swamp Canal Company shareholders and agents, the elections spawned rumors of disunion at the state and federal levels. Indeed, many white artisans in Richmond and in Norfolk joined Democratic Republican societies but felt that their interests were subordinated to those of party leaders, and these whites were not alone in feeling isolated from the benefits of liberty and equality. Among enslaved people in Virginia, a young and highly skilled blacksmith, Gabriel, politicized by the rhetoric of liberty and equality espoused by both Federalists and Democratic Republicans, saw a political and class divide and perceived the possibility of an impending civil war. Gabriel hoped to convince white artisans to join their urban enslaved counterparts in demanding justice, thereby exploiting the expanding rhetorical divide. The result was what historian Douglas Egerton has called the most extensive slave conspiracy in the history of the American South.[33]

In early August 1800, Gabriel and his co-conspirators plotted to overthrow Virginia's state government and demand the abolition of slavery. On the morning of August 30, however, county militias rounded up suspected conspirators, and on September 11, local magistrates began trials for conspiracy and insurrection. Over the following two months, almost seventy men were tried, forty-four were convicted, and twenty-seven, including Gabriel, were hanged.[34]

However, Gabriel's plot to bring racial equity by way of rebellion did not die the day he was taken to the gallows. During the fall of 1801, Sancho, held by John Booker of Amelia, revived Gabriel's plot. A ferryman, Sancho labored on the Roanoke River along the border between Halifax and Charlotte Counties, both of which had majority-black populations. Sancho devised a new plot to overthrow slavery in Virginia. He had not been directly involved in Gabriel's original plan, but in his travels, he had recruited conspirators near Petersburg to support the offensive against Richmond. Sancho took a number of lessons from Gabriel's failure, seeking a small, dedicated band of followers to lessen the chance that the plot would be betrayed and eschewing the idea of inspiring masses of disfranchised white artisans and laborers to join the cause. However, Sancho's co-conspirators—enslaved watermen hired out on the region's rivers—expected that "the poor [white] sort that has no blacks" would remain neutral during the uprising.[35]

By November, the core group numbered almost sixty, among them Humphrey, Abram, and Absalom. They uprising was planned for either Good Friday or Easter Monday 1802, though the date was kept secret. The plan was much simpler than Gabriel's scheme: the rebels would launch a quick strike against whites, beginning with a meeting at Daniel Dejarnett's pub and Jamison's store. By quickly dispatching slaveholding whites and those who sought to defend the counties, Sancho and the other conspirators expected to wrest concessions from local authorities: primarily freedom, but also the right to wages and an equitable distribution of property. They also hoped that the revolt would contribute to the decline of slavery throughout the Lower Chesapeake region by inspiring the watermen's wives, cousins, friends, and parents to abandon enslavement.[36]

The success of such a conspiracy would certainly have struck at the heart of the DSC's efforts to build sustainable operations in the Great Dismal on the backs of enslaved people. As DSC agents including John Driver, Thomas Shepherd, and Thomas Swepson knew well, enslaved rivermen provided a vital link not only among fall-line towns such as Richmond and Petersburg but also between Atlantic port towns including Norfolk, Portsmouth, and Suffolk. As they moved goods and information around the Lower Chesapeake region, these men also circulated news of enslaved people who attempted to overthrow the new American republic. Absalom carried news of the Halifax conspiracy to Charlotte County, while others brought the idea to Petersburg. By Christmas 1801, information regarding the scheme had reached Nottaway, bordering Amelia and Dinwiddie Counties in southeastern Virginia, where the ringleaders were Joe and Bob, enslaved by Batt Jones and John Royall. Joe and Bob planned to rally a group to slaughter whites in a quick strike against enslavement before marching on Petersburg, a plan similar to that envisioned by Sancho's men. Bob and Joe's men would then join with other groups at Halifax.[37]

But the plot quickly overextended. In Nottoway, Ned, enslaved by Grief Green, reported hearing four unfamiliar enslaved people speak regarding the conspiracy. In Petersburg, Rochester Jumper, a free man, recruited Lewis, an enslaved waterman who labored at the Manakin town ferry. Enslaved by John Brown, Lewis was hired to travel to Petersburg and did so under the authority of a pass he wrote for himself. Lewis carried the news of the conspiracy out of the Appomattox River basin as far as Goochland County, twenty miles north of Richmond. From Manakin, Lewis carried news of the conspiracy to Franke Goode, Roling Pointer, and Jacob Martin, literate enslaved people who took up the charge of leading the plot in Powhatan. Lewis then carried the plot to Richmond, where he found few recruits: memories of the fates of Gabriel and his co-conspirators remained fresh. Enslaved watermen also ferried news of the conspiracy down the James River to Norfolk, where enslaved blacks were more enthusiastic. By 1802, the port town was home to nearly seven thousand residents, almost three thousand of whom were black. A group of potential conspirators emerged centered around Will, enslaved by the estate of Mary and William Walke of neighboring Princess Anne County. The Walke heirs permitted Will to hire his time at the city's docks, where Will sought to recruit not only free and enslaved black laborers but also whites.[38]

As the primary port for the Lower Chesapeake, Norfolk hosted numerous black watermen from North Carolina. An "emissary" soon carried the plan to Elizabeth City, initiating a "correspondence" between that port town on the Pasquotank River and meetings in Norfolk. The conspiracy eventually reached further into northeastern North Carolina, penetrating Bertie, Halifax, Hertford, and Martin Counties. Information regarding the Halifax conspiracy also reached enslaved blacks in North Carolina via another channel. From Booker's Ferry in Virginia, Isaac, a skilled slave held by the estate of Joseph Wilkes, traveled down the Roanoke to Brunswick County, where he recruited Phill and charged him with raising a company of slaves. Isaac then continued down the Roanoke into North Carolina, taking news of the Halifax conspiracy to Roanoke Rapids, whence it spread to North Carolina's Halifax County. The North Carolina rebels perceived themselves as an extension of Sancho's plot. According to Davy, a literate slave, the "head negroes" lived in Virginia, "a negro man somewhere in Virg[ini]a" had orchestrated the plot "under the ground," and "when the fight was begun all the negroes were to join those who commenced." Many of the North Carolina blacks who pledged allegiance to the original plot were rivermen, like Sancho and Isaac, who were trusted to hire their own time for wages then conveyed to slaveholders. Many wanted more physical and economic independence than they could obtain as hired enslaved watermen. Some were like Salem, who told others that he envisioned a fight for the right to the full fruits of their labor and for control of their time. But despite the connections Isaac and others forged, the concerted, quick-striking, and broad-reaching revolt Sancho envisioned was not to be. The North Carolina rebels formed their own plot led by "Captain" King Brown and Frank, both of whom were literate, and slated to occur on June 10. Brown and Frank's men would set ablaze houses in the small village of Windsor and await new recruits from area plantations. When the others arrived, the group would march north to assist the Virginia rebels. By mid-spring 1802, King Brown and Frank had recruited nearly thirty leaders, each of whom pledged to form a group to execute the plan. On May 6, King Brown declared to another rebel that all insurgents along the Roanoke were poised to rise in revolt.[39]

As early as December 1801, Virginia authorities heard rumors of a new conspiracy and mobilized slave patrols near Petersburg. Sancho, living upriver from Petersburg, was unaware of the patrols and thus did not communicate a new plan of action to the conspirators at Nottaway, who continued to wait for the Easter holiday. But on January 1, 1802, patrols rounded up Bob, Joe, and three lieutenants, accusing them of actively planning a revolt. Bob revealed the plot, and Major Richard Jones relayed the news to Petersburg mayor William Prentis. The following day, Prentis initiated communication with Virginia governor James Monroe, and two weeks later, Monroe alerted the General Assembly, explaining that several causes had inspired the "growing sentiment of liberty" expressed by Virginia's enslaved people. Gabriel and Sancho and their followers had not been excited merely by their enslavement, warned Monroe, but also by the notions of liberty and equality voiced by white Virginians.[40]

About a week later, Bob and Joe were hanged in Nottoway, but Virginia authorities knew that they were not the originators of the revolt and continued to seek other conspirators. In early February, Isaac and Phill were arrested and hanged. The testimony against Isaac revealed that the plot had extended further than Virginia authorities had thought, and Norfolk mayor John Cowper reported to Monroe rumors regarding a revolt there. On April 15, Caleb Boush and Jarvis revealed Will's role; under questioning, Will implicated Ned and Jeremiah. More conspirators were arrested in Norfolk, and the local militia was called up to defend the city. The Easter holiday passed without incident as Sancho's plot unraveled.[41]

Acting on information provided by Abram, authorities arrested Sancho, who appeared in court on April 23. Abram declared that Sancho bore full responsibility for the plot and that Sancho had organized two companies to meet at Jameson's store the night before Easter. The justices swiftly sentenced Sancho to the gallows in three weeks' time. As the hanging date approached, Halifax authorities arrested Sancho's lieutenants, including Absalom, Frank, and Martin, and the four men as well as Abram were hanged on May 15. A total of thirteen enslaved people were tried in Halifax.[42]

As news of Sancho's execution reached North Carolina, Governor Benjamin Williams, mobilized the militia, which on June 2 intercepted a letter addressed to King Brown that listed the names of fourteen conspirators. By June 10, patrollers had rounded up more than thirty local bondmen and convinced two young enslaved boys to confess the extent of the plot. Those identified as the plot's leaders were sent to Windsor to stand trial, and on June 16, King Brown and nine others were hanged.[43]

The enslaved rivermen who joined Sancho's plot possessed an essential knowledge of the region's rivers and forests. Because their labors often meant long trips at great distances from the properties of the slaveholders who hired them out, these black rivermen possessed a degree of freedom that ultimately amounted to petit marronage. This was a key feature that distinguished Gabriel's group of conspirators, the majority of whom were skilled urban artisans, from most of those who joined Sancho's plot.[44]

Most—but not all. One of these skilled rivermen was Tom Copper, a maroon who led the North Carolina wing of Sancho's Easter Conspiracy. To local authorities near Elizabeth City, Copper was known as the General of the Swamps. From a hideout in the southern Dismal, Copper led raids on local plantations, reportedly tapping into the network of enslaved rivermen to coordinate his group's movements with the enslaved people who toiled on plantations within a hundred-mile radius. Through this form of petit marronage, Copper maintained his own freedom and facilitated liberty for the absconders who took refuge with him.[45]

By the first decade of the nineteenth century, enslaved people in the Dismal found themselves in a wetland drawn ever more closely into the early American republic via the port at Norfolk. And that republic was seeking its footing in late Atlantic world networks of exchange. Many enslaved Virginians and North Carolinians slipped into and out of the Great Dismal and other swamps and forests in the region, moving about between two landscapes of slavery as they engaged in petit marronage, a practice that caused some white Virginians and North Carolinians great apprehension. Virginia and North Carolina developed growing populations of free black people that also caused concern among whites. Prominent Virginians including Thomas Jefferson offered "solutions" to the state's free-black "problem," including diffusion and colonization in West Africa. In 1806, Virginia passed a measure that required newly manumitted blacks to leave the state within a year, and North Carolina passed similar legislation. But African Americans continued to resist control, with some remaining entrenched in local swamps and forests.

CHAPTER 3

"All Delinquents in Duty"
Petit Marronage and the Dismal Swamp Canal

In late July 1801, several weeks before Sancho revived Gabriel's plot to foment a revolt against Virginia's governing and political elites, commission merchant Richard Blow received a letter delivered by "old Bob," who had arrived in Portsmouth the previous night. Old Bob's trip was more than a simple one-way errand sanctioned by an enslaver's pass. The whites who imposed control on Old Bob's movements trusted that he not only would convey the missive in his possession but would return with a response. They also trusted that Bob and the coopers who accompanied him could be relied on to make a journey of at least forty miles without supervision, in the midst of broader unrest in the commonwealth.[1] While Blow made no mention of Gabriel's routed plot and could not yet know of the conspiracy being organized by Sancho and others, Blow affirmed his confidence in Bob in the midst of a yellow fever outbreak, the most pressing concern. Blow sent Old Bob to carry news of the outbreak to Petersburg, almost seventy-five miles northwest of Portsmouth.[2]

Though such confidence is compelling, neither Blow nor other commission merchants in the Lower Chesapeake region commonly sent letters by enslaved persons. Nevertheless, it is clear that on some occasions, enslaved people in the area traveled significant distances from their enslavers and returned to them. Old Bob's transit is also of interest because he and the coopers with whom he traveled passed through the greater Dismal Swamp region via Suffolk.

In addition to his commission merchant business, Blow held stock in the Dismal Swamp Canal Company (DSCC). As a shareholder, Blow was well aware that the DSCC, along with the Dismal Swamp Company (DSC) and other outfits, regularly dispatched enslaved labor crews into the swamp, a landscape that also included nearby maroon camps. Yet despite the existence of such settlements, Blow trusted Old Bob not to take advantage of his proximity and lack of supervision to vanish among the swamp's maroons. What can the limited archive of Old Bob's labors as Blow's letter carrier, combined with the fuller records of the DSC and the DSCC, tell us about petit marronage and the Lower Chesapeake's informal and extractive economy? By 1805, that economy was anchored by four constituent bodies—Blow and his agent at Deep Creek, Virginia, Samuel Proctor, who was employed by the DSCC; the DSC; the Bear Quarter Company; and the DSCC—that cooperated to expand access to the swamp by creating the Dismal Swamp Canal. The Great Canal, as it came to be known, would change the swamp's eastern fringe. In pursuit of their ultimate aim of turning a profit in the swamp, Blow and Proctor joined earlier DSC shareholders, managers, and agents in tacitly accepting petit marronage as a vital component of company operations.

The practical work of ignoring petit marronage fell on the shoulders of Proctor and other white swamp agents who acted on behalf of shareholders' interests at slave labor camps. In so doing, these agents also established their own livelihoods and provided for their families. They also tacitly facilitated slave labor camps that provided key resources for maroons who claimed the swamp as a place of refuge.

❧

To compel enslaved laborers to dig the largest of swamp infrastructure projects, the Dismal Swamp Canal, DSCC officials engaged the local custom of tacit acceptance of petit marronage. Championed by Virginia governor Patrick Henry as early as 1784, the Dismal Swamp Canal was chartered by Virginia Assembly on December 1, 1787. However, canal construction could not begin until North Carolina passed a similar act, which did not occur until November 1790. Construction of the canal then began at Deep Creek three years later. Between 1794 and 1805, several hundred enslaved laborers hacked away at dense undergrowth, felled large trees, dug up deep root systems, and carved into the swamp's boggy ground the first stage of the canal, which traversed twenty-two miles of pocosin and pine forest to

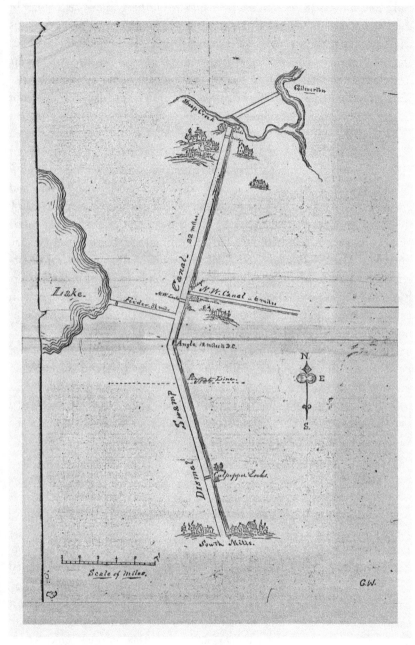

Map of the Dismal Swamp Canal, ca. 1812. Business Records Collection, accession 26665, Library of Virginia, Richmond.

the Pasquotank River in North Carolina, the canal's southern terminus. Between 1807 and 1812, a second phase of slave labor deepened and lengthened the waterway. During the third phase, enslaved laborers cut a six-mile canal to the Northwest River in North Carolina, connecting the Dismal Swamp Canal to the Currituck Sound. Enslaved laborers also cut a 3.5-mile feeder ditch to the west, linking the canal to Lake Drummond. The feeder canal enabled the waters of Lake Drummond to be used to control the water level of the main canal. By its completion in 1829, the Dismal Swamp Canal effectively facilitated a sheltered inland water route that connected the Chesapeake Bay to the Elizabeth River in Portsmouth and on to the Albemarle Sound via the Pasquotank River. Before the late 1820s, the Dismal Swamp Canal was navigable only by shingle flats and small lighters. After the DSCC dispatched slave laborers to widen and deepen the waterway, the Great Canal was opened to vessels with up to a 5.5-foot draft.[3]

Richard Blow's letterbooks contain notations regarding how each letter reached its destination. In some instances, Blow recorded the enslaved letter carrier's name, though in other cases he did not. Blow conducted business in a number of important commodities—most commonly tobacco, pork, cotton, and salt—and frequently needed to send letters to factors near and far. Blow's wharves warehoused, imported, or shipped barrel staves, shingles, lumber, tar, turpentine, herring, Indian corn, sugar, flour, and Irish potatoes, and he commissioned cargoes for at least seven vessels—the *Venus*, the *Rebecca*, the *Averick*, the *Vancours*, the *Niagara*, the *Lacona*, and the *Argus*—that connected Blow's operations to a regional economy centered in Virginia's James, York, and Rappahannock River Valleys. These vessels also connected the Virginia Southside and northeastern North Carolina to planters, farmers, and small merchants in Virginia's riverine network; to the new nation's major ports in New York, Charleston, and Baltimore; and to major Atlantic world ports in Jamaica, Bermuda, Liverpool, London, Cork, and Rotterdam.

Prior to 1815, Blow regularly enlisted Old Bob and others to carry letters. Subsequently, however, changing sentiments regarding free blacks' mobility in the region seem to have begun to give Blow pause. Perhaps the widespread fears provoked by the slave conspiracies of 1802 that led Virginia lawmakers to restrict manumission also tempered Blow's trust in Old Bob. On January 7, 1806, Blow wrote to Thomas Newton of Norfolk regarding two concerns: a slave named Robin and Newton's offer to hire to the company a number of "fellows" on annual contracts. Blow reported that although no final decision had been made, the DSCC directors were hesitant to accept Newton's proposal because one particular laborer had been "a runaway for some time past." Regarding Robin, however, Blow expected a decision within the week and had "no doubt" that "Negro Robin" would "be continued as heretofore."[4]

Evidence that some enslaved people hired by the DSCC fled Blow's forced labor camp to engage in petit marronage is not surprising. But other letters suggest that the canal attracted enslaved people to seek to labor in the swamp. On January 21, 1806, Blow informed Richard S. Green that "your man Harry has come over for the purpose of going on the Canal," perhaps having heard of the relative latitude, compared with that of slaves in other contexts, that canal laborers enjoyed. Blow was primarily concerned with protecting himself from responsibility if Harry became ill while at the canal camp: Harry would need a blanket, and Blow "therefore thought best to send him back to you for the purpose of getting one or two, or if you wish me to find them & deduct them from his wages, youll please say so by his return in the morning."[5] The rising demand for enslaved laborers for the canal meant that Blow was amenable to Harry's request, while Blow's actions—sending Harry to obtain supplies and expecting him to return—demonstrate that Blow not only wanted Green to bear the burden of provisioning Harry but also that both white men trusted him not to run away.

Several letters from Blow to Proctor reveal more clearly the conditions at the canal site, suggest the persistence of petit marronage in the Dismal, and provide evidence that swamp agents saw their roles as offering opportunities to advance their position in white southern society. On January 21, 1806, Blow noted that he had received a letter from Proctor "by the Negroes who brought it down" but took issue with the fact that they apparently had not done so in a timely manner: "They only called and delivered it as they were going up, which is very wrong." In the future, whenever Proctor entrusted a letter to "any of them again, direct-them to call with the letter to me as soon as they come here, and if I am at not home to leave it at my house."[6] Blow instructed Proctor to keep a strict accounting of provisions sent for canal laborers: "My young man has sent up by Tow to you 8 pair Shoes for the Negroes who want them," but the costs were to "be deducted from their wages." Those wages were not paid to the slaves themselves but to the slaveholders from whom they had been hired. Blow also directed Proctor to give the canal laborers "strict orders, at what time they are to be at their places of work every monday morning" and to make sure that they were compelled to labor no more than one hour after they arrived "without a reasonable & good excuse." In addition to tardiness, absence was apparently a problem: Blow had heard that "Jim Pennock has not been up since christmast," and Pennock's exact whereabouts were unknown. If Proctor saw him "lurking about Norfolk," Blow wanted to be informed so "that I may have him taken up & sent to you, by a constable." Blow also advised Proctor to seek further guidance about how to deal with other laborers who resisted work. Blow explained that a "young fellow name Henry" had been hired from a Norfolk enslaver. Henry "appears to have been brought up tenderly, never been used to hard work," and his owner wanted him taught the ways of slave labor. Proctor, therefore, should "see if [Henry] will answer our purpose." If so, Proctor should keep him at the site. But if Henry refused, Proctor should "let him return home with a letter to me."[7]

Finally, Blow instructed Proctor to allow each laborer to imbibe one dram of liquor in the morning, a practice that was "contrary to former usage." Proctor had previously been discouraged from allowing the canal laborers to drink at all, but a small amount was now permitted to encourage good behavior. If the spirit rations did not produce the desired result, "all delinquents in Duty" would be denied "their allowance." Despite such labor issues, Blow remained confident that the canal project would be carried out and retained his trust in his enslaved letter carriers: groups of "canal negroes" would be carrying the letter to Proctor in the swamp.[8]

Between 1807 and 1808, the canal project was fraught with inefficiencies, many of them caused by the enslaved laborers. For example, in mid-January 1807, Blow explained that although he had received a letter delivered "by the negro man" Proctor sent, the man had not arrived until the late evening and could not be sent to Norfolk to retrieve the requested supplies until the following morning. In the morning, however, the laborer "went off," and Blow "did not see or hear any more of him." The materials' delayed arrival at the swamp would hinder progress toward the goal of "opening a way to" Lake Drummond by the following week.[9] On one level, this letter signals the operations of an efficient enterprise: a dutiful agent overseeing the construction of the Dismal Swamp Canal, and an equally dutiful merchant ensuring the transportation of necessary supplies between Norfolk, Portsmouth, and the canal construction site. But the enterprise's efficiency was tenuous at best and could be disrupted when a single enslaved laborer seized on the relative freedom of his duty.

Four months later, Blow told Proctor that the "Bear Quarter Gentlemen" would be sending some enslaved laborers to the canal for "a few weeks" to expedite construction during a period of good weather. The Bear Quarter Company would benefit from the effort, since an unobstructed canal would enable shingles to be floated freely to the canal's main branch.[10] Within a few days, however, Blow learned that the Bear Quarter Company had refused to send Proctor the laborers. Blow then sent "negro Robin" to Proctor with another letter advising him to proceed with the canal construction as he saw fit. Blow also directed Proctor to retaliate against Bear Quarter: "If the shingle gitters wont join you with their hands to clear it out, and attempt to carry the shingles across the canal, you may easily prevent them by taking up the Bridges."[11] In July 1808, Blow again lamented his inability to send Proctor more enslaved laborers and again suggested that Proctor solicit help from the Bear Quarter people, who would benefit from having the canal cleared.[12]

Blow's other operations as a commission merchant offer insight into how the maroons who worked in the swamp sustained themselves and how the swamp's internal economy functioned.[13] In December 1808, Blow was engaged in a dispute with Lewis Bond, who was not only refusing to pay a bill for an 1805 shipment of pork but was arguing that Blow was indebted to him for having failed to collect satisfactory proceeds on the shipment. Blow had been under the impression that he was to sell the pork on commission and had paid Bond a thousand dollars, which reflected a satisfactory payment minus the commission. Blow did not explain his reasons for his confidence, and in the ensuing three years, he had also failed to retail the pork to either enslaved Dismal Swamp shingle getters or to tradesmen in Norfolk or Portsmouth; what little had been sold had gone to vessels at port in Norfolk. To answer Bond's claim, Blow explained that he was still out more than $650 on the pork.[14]

The dispute between Blow and Bond provides information regarding the Lower Chesapeake region's diversifying economy in the wake of the deepening devaluation of tobacco. By the early nineteenth century, both planters and merchants had shifted emphasis away from tobacco to a broader range of crops and commodities, with pork, wheat, and shingles predominating in Southside Virginia.[15] Blow's letterbooks also illustrate the ways that Proctor built a materially successful life out of the same swamp in which enslaved laborers toiled for sparse material gain. In so doing, these and other documents help to explain why both men tacitly permitted petit marronage at the canal site after his tenure as Blow's swamp agent.

By March 1816, Samuel Proctor was employed by the DSC, a capacity in which he was responsible for apprising shareholders of developments in the swamp. Writing from Deep Creek, Virginia, on March 12, 1816, Proctor advised James Henderson, "Your timber laying in the Dismal Swamp Canal are much exposed to pilage. I think if you had some good person—working the timber they would prevent others from pillaging—which are much Practiced at present." Proctor further suggested that Henderson "be very cautious—who you suffer to work—as we have a number of broken merchants down here at this time." Those "broken merchants," likely included competing speculators and unsanctioned enslaved shingle getters and enslaved canal cutters engaged in petit marronage. Proctor viewed such people as potential pillagers of timber and believed that "no contract made with them would be of any device." Moreover, Proctor cautioned that "it will be well for you to enquire into the character and sercumstances of those you admit to work." He always offered such advice to "persons living at a distance—and holding property in the canal," since "being always on the Spot—I see every thing that is going on."[16] It is noteworthy that Proctor did not, however, explicitly mention maroons as among the perils that might threaten the interests of the DSC shareholders.

Discharging his duties as the company's "faithful servant," Proctor again wrote to Henderson a week later, estimating that ten to fifteen enslaved shingle getters were responsible for the missing timber. Pillage was a "strange kind of business" pursued by a certain "class of people." Proctor suggested that the DSC hire "some good person . . . whose business and interest it would be to be constantly in—and about your swamp." He recommended the employment of William West to oversee a camp of eighteen to twenty "hands."[17] Although Henderson apparently heeded Proctor's advice to hire trustworthy contractors, progress on the construction of the canal did not meet shareholders' goals or solve the issue of pillaged timber. In late June 1817, Proctor reported a delay in surveying because the company lacked the court order that would permit it to commence. Proctor nevertheless remained optimistic: despite the recent rains, shingles produced in the swamp could be sold for ten dollars a board, and he could obtain seventeen thousand of the best quality shingles.[18]

Another letter from Proctor, written more than a year later, reveals that the DSC remained enmeshed in land disputes with Edwin Sexton, John Bartee, and Robert Butt. Bartee and Butt had assured Proctor that they would not cut more timber until the dispute was resolved but had reneged, delegating the labor to "other persons who are cutting & carving off all in their power" and "will cut all that is of any value." Proctor saw the situation as urgent: "You had better seek some remedy if there is any." Wilby Foreman, Isaac Wallace, and Wilson Bartee of the Bear Quarter Company were eager to buy an interest in the timber and determined to produce shingles at the site, and only dramatic measures would stop them: Proctor suggested taking "the water . . . entirely out of the DS Canal." Doing so would mean that the new purchasers "cannot bring any shingles this way and by prohibiting them comeing down your Canal will finally stop them untill next winter."[19]

In January 1819, however, Proctor reported that the problems continued. One of the Norfolk County surveyors had "not done any thing in the companys swamp since March 1817," and the other, William West, had been at work "only at such times as when the water was drown out the canal for the purpose of working on it." And West's work proceeded "with a much less number of hands than specified in his Contract." In addition to the complications caused by competing land claims, the company still owed back taxes on its land. When Proctor began work for the DSC nearly three years earlier, he had expected the taxes to be paid "as heretofore done as you have other lands in this neighbourhood." But despite the fact that such taxes were not his responsibility, "if the compy requires it I will pay the taxes on this land or any other they may have in this county and will inquire into the thing in and see it is paid." Finally, he again advised the shareholders to "get some person to work whose business it would be to be on the land for it lays in a neighbourhood very much exsposed to pillage"—precisely the role that Proctor had assumed for Richard Blow ten years earlier. Proctor thought that "a quantity of the second quality shingles might be got on it yet" if the price were reduced significantly.[20]

No competing partner would institute such a dramatic price reduction, so Proctor was in effect suggesting that the labor be hired out to an independent contractor, though he did not name one. That he failed to do so introduces a new possibility: hiring the "pillagers" who had long plagued the company. "Pillage," with its connotations of actions by an extralegal body of people, invokes the possibility that Proctor was suggesting implicitly that the company hire maroons. By this time, increasing numbers of enslaved blacks toiled in the Dismal, which was more open to the regional riverine economy and through it to the Atlantic world. Nevertheless, Proctor's reluctance to state explicitly the laborers to whom he referred indicates that the swamp's internal economies of exchange had yet to give up all secrets.

The Dismal's maroons, unlike their counterparts in other swamps and forests of the Atlantic world, had not built a permanent physical community that outsiders could document or chart but instead were sustained by petit marronage. Petit marronage enabled the Dismal maroons to remain outside the more traditional context of black enslavement in Virginia and North Carolina, but why would that have been of interest to Proctor or the Dismal Swamp Company? In late 1820, Proctor signaled a significant shift in his position regarding the production of swamp shingles. This change reflected the development of the regional shingle economy, which was becoming increasingly dependent on the Dismal's maroons. Frustrated by the DSC's quarrels with its rivals, Proctor reported to shareholders that "the managers of your Company was so indecisive in respect to leting out the Timber owned by them & E. Sexton they declared there Willingness to let out this timber by contract." But more than a year later, contracting the labor to produce shingles continued to present a challenge, and "no application in all this length of time had been made which is enough to convince them that that method will not do." Moreover, "from the little allarm given by threattening to sue the former contracters, the common class of people such as buys there timber by the thousand has become shy & timid." Proctor no longer saw himself as among that "common class of people," and he had moved further away from the deferential language that characterized his earlier correspondence with DSC shareholders. Proctor now advocated that the DSC assume a role as the authority that set the price for timber in the swamp region, holding out "no other terror or restrait" against the people "but to pay for the timber as they git the shingles and sell them."[21]

Proctor's new approach would have important consequences for local whites, who had long participated in a regional riverine economy that had resisted market prices determined by incorporated companies at the behest of Atlantic markets. Such a sea change also threatened to transform how maroons engaged in the swamp's informal exchange economy, in turn potentially hindering merchants' and land companies' efforts to construct the swamp's infrastructure and the DSC's efforts to produce shingles. According to Proctor, becoming a price-setting authority would cause enough local people to work under terms set by the company that the it could create binding contractual agreements with competing outfits in the swamp. "The first one that neglects or fails to pay for the timber on the day he sells & receives the money for the shingles sold" would no longer have employment with the DSC. Proctor saw quick action as necessary, writing, "If you do not go to work Mr Sexton will and suggesting that prices be set at $125 for two-foot boards and $250 for three-foot boards."[22]

These prices—exponentially higher than those Proctor suggested three years earlier—may indicate that the region had begun to recover from the economic upheavals that had upset local and national confidence in the early republic's nascent financial system during the Panic of 1819.[23] Such prices also had the potential to provide the company with significant profits, which, in turn, could be used to further develop the Dismal Swamp and hire more slaves. This meant trouble for the swamp's maroons, who would have been compelled to retreat deeper into swamp to escape the encroaching canals and lumbering companies.

Before 1820, the DSC's and DSCC's efforts to construct timber camps and internal improvements in the swamp were limited in scope. The resulting paucity of sources revealing the details of Proctor's interactions with enslaved canal cutters and/or maroons hinders efforts to paint a fuller picture of the Dismal's internal slave economy in the early Republican period. Nevertheless, the extant sources provide ample evidence of petit marronage even as company efforts portended significant change in the Dismal's landscape. The growth of the two companies' footprints in the swamp threatened the refuge the swamp had offered its maroon residents. The most dramatic of these changes occurred along the swamp's eastern fringe, where the DSCC worked to improve the Great Canal, but changes also occurred elsewhere. The DSC continued to dispatch enslaved shingle getters to new timber camps in other sectors, bringing the deeper, more remote sectors of the swamp—and the maroons who inhabited those areas—into closer contact with the Virginia Southside and the outside world. Richard Blow, Samuel Proctor, and other swamp developers sought to impose their vision on a landscape that was already claimed and utilized by a host of different peoples. These men largely ignored the maroons except when petit marronage became outright flight, as in the case of Jim Pennock, or when they could benefit the developers by serving as a market for excess commodities such as pork. The DSC subsequently increased its investments in swamp infrastructure, leading to more camps of slave and freed black laborers at the same time that the transatlantic antislavery movement was gaining strength amid national debates in the United States regarding slavery's perpetuation and spread into the western territories. Abolitionist writers sought to expose slavery's weaknesses by bringing national attention to the peculiar institution's anomalies in the form of the Dismal's shingle and canal camps, where petit marronage persisted.

As a primary facilitator of commission merchant and land company interests in developing the swamp, Proctor often found that the only way to further company goals was to concede to the demands of enslaved laborers and perhaps maroons. In so doing, he benefited personally. His last will and testament, written in Camden County, North Carolina, in March 1831, listed substantial amounts of property. He owned seven different land tracts in Virginia and North Carolina; a house and lot in Elizabeth City, North Carolina, and in Deep Creek, Virginia; a house and farming implements at his home plantation; and various swamper's tools acquired during his years of toil in the Dismal. Proctor had two land claims along the Dismal Swamp Canal, including a 145-acre plot on the canal's west side "commencing at Spence's Road & extending up the canal" to the Culpepper Lock. In addition, Proctor directed that "my negroes . . . be equally divided between my five children" and his wife.[24] Proctor had risen from the life of a swamper to a life of considerable material wealth, in the process becoming a slaveholder.

Like Old Bob, Robin, and other enslaved persons who can be glimpsed in archival documents, Proctor lived in multiple contexts, including one characterized by local merchants who sought to open the swamp's natural resources to the broader Atlantic world and one characterized by enslaved laborers who, when engaged in petit marronage, reflected the region's long heritage of black resistance. Unlike Proctor, canal slaves lacked the ability to pursue paths to lives of freedom. Still, as was true elsewhere in Virginia and North Carolina as well as throughout the South, whites and blacks interacted locally in the Dismal, shaping race and enslavement in ways that often contradicted state and federal laws. Such interactions ensured that petit marronage benefited all who acquiesced to its existence and would endure until the early years of the Civil War.

CHAPTER 4

"To Manage the Business of the Swamp"

*The Informal Slave Economy, Freedom, and
Unfreedom in the Great Dismal Swamp*

First published in London in 1843 and reprinted in three Boston editions by abolitionist Oliver Johnson in 1844, the narrative of Moses Grandy was perhaps the first widely distributed firsthand account of the particular circumstances of slavery in the Great Dismal Swamp. As Grandy took to lecterns before abolitionist audiences in New England, he articulated the stories of enslaved laborers, of the extreme conditions in which canals and timber were cut, and of the region's extractive and informal slave economies. "The ground is often very boggy," Grandy explained, and slaves' bodies were covered "up to the middle, or much deeper, in mud and water," with labor continuing as long as they were able to "keep their heads above water." For overnight shelter, company slaves camped in huts made of shingles and boards, often lying in the mud by the fireside to ward off biting insects with little more than a blanket for warmth. Company agents visited the sites monthly, sometimes providing laborers with meager cash payments that were turned over to enslavers. Other times, agents distributed tobacco or other rations that had been approved by company officials to encourage slaves to continue their labors.[1]

At the time the narrative was published, Grandy estimated himself to be about fifty-six years old. Born in 1786 or 1787 in Camden County, North Carolina, Grandy poignantly described his unbreakable commitment to purchasing his own freedom from several enslavers. His first enslaver, Billy Grandy, was a "hard-drinking man" who regularly sold enslaved people, including several of Moses's siblings, into the domestic slave trade. In the effort to prevent Billy Grandy from selling her children, Moses's mother often hid them in local forests, where she taught them to strain the water they sourced in puddles to remove impurities and where they learned from their mother to gather berries and to collect potatoes and raw corn from the farm.

Billy Grandy died when Moses was eight, and he was transferred to Billy's son, James, who was two days older than Moses. Until he was old enough to be "put to field work," the two boys played together, much as Thomas Jefferson played with the future enslaved valet, Jupiter.[2] Once old enough, Moses was hired out locally each January until he was twenty one, in keeping with the local practice of auction at the Camden County courthouse. For several years, Moses was hired out to Richard Furley, who paid the Grandy family between seventy and ninety dollars annually for Moses's labor. Furley permitted Moses to hire his own time, an arrangement that cost Moses as much as thirty dollars a year plus the amount that Furley owed the Grandy family. When James Grandy came of age, he, too, permitted Moses to hire out his own time but charged Moses as much as sixty dollars annually.

The two men came of age as Norfolk merchants faced the consequences of the Embargo Act of 1807, which President Thomas Jefferson signed in the effort to protect the U.S. merchant marine from increasing British impressments on the high seas. From December 1807 to March 1809, the embargo disrupted overseas trade, with vessels sitting idle in American ports, including Norfolk.[3] In the effort to avoid the Royal Navy's patrols of the Chesapeake, Norfolk merchants diverted cargoes to Elizabeth City, North Carolina, by way of the Dismal Swamp Canal. Ever industrious, Moses piloted some of these cargoes, sharing half of the money he earned with Charles Grice. Moses also hired other enslaved watermen to help him move boats along the canal. He used remainder of his earnings to purchase his freedom from James Grandy, paying him six hundred dollars in accordance with their agreement. But James reneged, eventually selling Moses to a man named Trewitt for six hundred dollars. Trewitt agreed to allow Moses to purchase his freedom for another six hundred dollars. Moses spent another two and a half years piloting cargoes along the Dismal Canal and saved up the money, but unbeknownst to him, Trewitt pledged Moses as collateral for a loan. Distraught after learning of this second betrayal, Moses fled into the swamp, hiding there until his new owner agreed to allow Moses to purchase his freedom. Yet once again, the enslaver failed to abide by those terms, transferring Moses to Enoch Sawyer, who also enslaved Moses's second wife.

Economy: Enslaved→(by DSC?) Monitored
Governed ↗ Ruled

Moses lightered shingles in the Dismal and hired enslaved swampers to assist his efforts. When Sawyer's two sons-in-law failed in their business in Norfolk, Sawyer sold eighteen slaves, his share of the Dismal, and two plantations but kept Moses and compelled him to plant corn. The two men agreed that Moses would pay Sawyer $230 and that his labors would earn him $8.00 a month toward the purchase of his freedom, but Sawyer refused to negotiate a total amount. After eight months, Moses received a pass to travel to Norfolk to seek employment with local merchants, but having learned his lesson, Moses instead sought help from Edward Minor at Deep Creek. In March 1827, the two men returned to Sawyer, and Minor paid $650 to purchase Moses.

still indebted

For the next three years, Moses Grandy piloted boats along the Dismal Swamp Canal to repay Minor, contracting rheumatism from exposure. To recover, Grandy marooned himself along the shore of Lake Drummond, where he received provisions from the enslaved shinglers with whom he bartered whenever "opportunity served." For shelter, he built a hut from juniper timber. As was the for many camps constructed by swamp slaves, it "was entirely open on one side" and was guarded at night by a campfire. According to Grandy, "One night I was awoke by some large animal smelling my face, and snuffing strongly; I felt its cold muzzle. I suddenly thrust out my arms, and shouted with all my might; it was frightened and made off. I do not know whether it was a bear or a panther, but it seemed as tall as a large calf."[4] In 1830, Grandy repaid Minor and moved to Providence, Rhode Island. He briefly returned to North Carolina but settled in Boston by 1840, when the city directory listed him as a laborer.[5]

escape finally

Though Grandy eventually earned his freedom and moved to New England and most of the Lower Chesapeake's enslaved shinglers and maroons never left the area, his account offers a firsthand look at what their lives were like. Moreover, in the course of Grandy's lifetime, the Dismal Swamp changed significantly from the swamp that earlier Dismal maroons—such as Tom or the black furniture maker—used as refuge, becoming much less remote as the Dismal Swamp Company (DSC), the Dismal Swamp Canal Company (DSCC), and smaller outfits expanded their footprints. Tracing these changes, this chapter examines the ways in which swamp agents Thomas Swepson and Frederick Hall stewarded the DSC's enterprises, thereby providing more details regarding slave labor at Dismal Swamp Land Company (DSLC) and DSCC camps. Although these documents offer insight into the lives of enslaved shingle getters as a group, the extant materials do not provide any information about these laborers as individuals: prior to the mid-1830s, DSC officials' correspondence did not note names or physical descriptions.

In February 1815, thirteen months before his formal appointment as a company agent, slave labor camp overseer Frederick Hall explained to DSC president James Henderson the terms under which Hall was assuming duties passed along by Suffolk agent Thomas Swepson. Swepson had closed his remaining accounts and paid four hundred dollars to Hall, part of which went to purchase "a little Pork and a few barrells of Corn for the hands."[6] On January 11, 1816, having officially accepted the post of DSC agent, Hall wrote again to Henderson, summarizing the company's affairs in the swamp and promising to "use every means in my power to manage the business of the swamp" to the company's advantage. Hall reviewed some personnel matters and estimated expenses for the coming year. Subsistence goods to sustain the company's slave labor camps would include pork at between $9.50 and $10.00 per hundred and corn at $4.50 per barrel. The cost of hiring "good shingle gitters" would range between eighty and ninety dollars per contract. The price for producing three-foot shingles would be four dollars per load. The company would pay nine dollars per load to have shingles transported to the canal and between four and six dollars per load to have the shingles floated down the canal on lighters. Hall anticipated that the company would need as many as sixty lighters.[7] Slave labor was key to all of these operations.

In 1815, the company had produced more than 1,000,000 three-foot shingles, 542,000 of which had been sold, 81,000 of which remained at the shingle yard, and 372,000 of which remained in the swamp. Given the balance of shingles from the previous season, Hall anticipated a boost in spring 1816 sales, but competition from other shingling outfits again threatened the DSC's yield. To mitigate against loss to competition, Swepson had advised Hall to employ ten to twelve enslaved shinglers at Lake Drummond, next to the ditch to Deep Creek, thereby establishing the company's presence in contested land and preventing "the deep Creek hands" from working timber on the company's claim. Finally, Hall turned to his compensation. Company managers had offered to let him "work three hands upon old refused Timber," the same way the company had compensated Swepson. Swepson, however, reported that he had been allowed to oversee four enslaved shinglers.[8]

At around this time, Swepson wrote to Henderson, commending Hall's "honesty, industry, and punctuality." Swepson then proposed that as a "peacable neighbour," he be permitted to oversee enslaved shinglers on "the remnant of Juniper timber" on company lands to the west of the Dismal Swamp Canal. Swepson had long had his eye on this juniper tract, and now sought to strike a bargain with the company that would result in a contract that would permit him to hire enslaved shingle getters who would be compelled to labor on company lands.[9] Less than a month later, Swepson wrote again, protesting the company managers' proposed prices for the juniper stand: such prices were "more than could be given were the timber of the best quality, unless there was a certainty of a continued Demand at good prices." Swepson countered by asking whether the company would consider "a reasonable compensation for trouble & risque" related to the "costs of each thousand shingles when delivered." Swepson suggested that he could deliver three-foot shingles at $10.00 per thousand, two-foot shingles at $5.50 per thousand, and twenty-one and eighteen-inch shingles at $4.00 per thousand; the company or its agent could then sell the shingles.[10]

Swepson's attempts to negotiate a contract with the DSC continued into March, when he explained to Henderson that he would not contract to oversee work in the juniper tract under traditional terms because doing so would require him to bear more than one thousand dollars in costs related to bridge construction and the purchase of carts, horses, and tools. Because the company refused to agree to terms that he found acceptable, Swepson advised Henderson "to look out elsewhere for employment for your hands & carts."[11] Hall's and Swepson's correspondence suggests that both men oversaw a considerable number of enslaved shingle getters and enslaved canal laborers and sought to increase those numbers to grow the company's imprint in the swamp.

Other parties, including Edwin Sexton and Daniel Williams and William West, also expressed interest in reaching agreements with the DSC in the spring of 1816. Williams and West were willing to pay no more than $4.50 per thousand for three-foot shingles and $1.50 for two-footers. The partners encouraged the company to approve their hire of at least thirty enslaved shinglers, though the exact number would be left "Blank in the Contract."[12] The request that the company set no limit on the number of enslaved shinglers it permitted its contractors to hire is evidence of a new, open-ended strategy intended to get the company to increase the number of slaves in the swamp to increase production of forest products. And as that number grew, so did the number of enslaved people who slipped away from company sites to more remote maroon camps.

Another pair of contractors, Matthew Spencer and Stephen Spencer, sought to purchase or to facilitate the cutting of juniper timber on a tract north of Lake Drummond. The Spencers proposed to pay five dollars per thousand for three-foot shingles, with amounts in "proportion" for two-footers, bolts, and split timber. They specifically targeted "left or refused" juniper, most likely positioning themselves as a secondary market for the more than 370,000 shingles left over from the 1815 season. To direct their efforts to a new land tract seemed impractical, as "a hand cannot perform the same task in the same time, as in a Swamp that has never been worked, and consequently would demand a greater price for making shingles."[13] The Spencers, too, did not reach an agreement with the DSC.[14]

Swepson continued to write to Henderson to express support of Hall's decisions—and to press the company to enter contracts that would be to Swepson's advantage. In January 1817, Swepson declared that Hall had reached lighterage terms for the coming season that would benefit the company "in conformity with the Resolution of the Managers," before suggesting that the DSC purchase a strategically located three-hundred-acre tract that he owned. Purchased at "a great bargain," the land lay "at the head of Managers mill run" and extended to the Norfolk line. Swepson was confident that the land would resell at a profit since it was "loaded with pine & cypress trees." Further, Swepson's land adjoined a tract owned by Thomas Shepherd the company could buy to create even more strategic value.[15] The company evidently turned down this proposal as well: Swepson's parcel was close to Riddick's Ditch and could not be definitively surveyed or marked without conflict with the Riddicks.[16]

By 1817, then, the encroachments facing the DSC had become increasingly organized. The Bear Quarter Company, the Riddicks, and others with long-standing claims to swamp tracts were joined by newcomers hoping to cash in by selling services or timber to the DSC. And all of these operators relied on enslaved shinglers, meaning that additional company agents were needed to oversee operations.

Between 1815 and 1820, Hall submitted regular reports to company officials, documenting growth in the company's operations overseen by managers and agents, conflicts with competing timber outfits operating on tracts adjacent to the DSC's claims, and growth in infrastructure, particularly canals and wooden roads. These changes resulted in part from shareholders' increased interest in profiting from the company's swamp investments. In January 1817, shareholder David Meade posed several questions pertaining to the company's swamp operations: Did any unsold shingles remain on hand at Suffolk or in the swamp, and if so, how many? How much money had shingles sales brought in? Had the company's Suffolk agent "employed as many hands as usual" in 1816, and had they been "chiefly occupied in making shingles, cleaning canal," or other tasks? What was the current price of shingles? And perhaps most important, how much of a dividend would shareholders receive in the coming spring?[17]

At the start of the shingle season in February, Hall noted that between twenty-five and thirty enslaved shingle getters were sent into a DSC claim to cut and produce three-foot shingles. Ten remained along the canal's banks to receive the shingles before lighters floated them north to Suffolk.[18] In March, Hall reported to Henderson that Mills Riddick had begun operations along the southern shore of Lake Drummond on February 26. Hall had traveled to the site and spent several days surveying and marking the company's land with the assistance of enslaved shingle getters. Hall observed a crew of at least thirteen enslaved shinglers whom Riddick had dispatched to a land tract more than a quarter of a mile in size near company claims. Working in this tract during the previous year, these men had "cut and worked up a considerable quantity of your prime Timber"—more than one hundred thousand three- and two-foot shingles. Hall subsequently "drove [Riddick's] hands off" and then went to Riddick himself and "forbid his moving or counting a shingle on the rode." Hall also declared that he would not permit Riddick's lighters to float along the Dismal Swamp Canal. Riddick assured Hall that no lighters would be sent down the canal and promised to tell the crew at the Lake Drummond shingle camp to end its operations. Hall requested instructions for how to handle the shingles the Riddick crew had left to rot and noted that the company should have "as many shingle gitters at work this year as we shall be able to manage."[19] Perhaps not surprisingly, Riddick may not have instructed his crew on the south shore of Lake Drummond to end its operations. On March 23, Hall wrote that Josiah and Mills Riddick "know well the line" that divided the southwestern sector of the swamp from the DSC's claim to the northeast. Moreover, according to Hall, the Riddicks' "long absence from their shingle gitters strengthens the presumption that they at least believed or suspected, that their people were doing wrong and that they did not like themselves to witness the evil done."[20]

In mid-April, Hall reported that he had invited the Riddicks to jointly survey the disputed sector, but they did not accept.[21] Hall continued his efforts to defend the DSC's claims over the following weeks at the same time that the company's efforts to produce shingles expanded. In late June, Hall wrote that he was managing "a set a bout 30 hands" on the bank of the canal, whose labors included hacking away at the underbrush that regularly threatened to consume its banks. Over the preceding thirty-six hours, rains had raised the water level in the canal nine inches, and Hall hoped that continued rains would enable company lighters to float along the canal within a few days as well as slow a recent natural fire that threatened the company's operations.[22]

Despite these challenges, Hall reported positive earnings by late November. At the end of the first quarter, Hall had paid the company treasurer eight thousand dollars, with shingles holding steady at twenty dollars per thousand. The price of shingles subsequently fell to eighteen dollars per thousand, where it remained through September and October. Hall expected the proceeds for the most recent quarter to amount to five thousand dollars. With work suspended through Christmas, Hall anticipated good sales in the spring of 1817 and "a handsome dividend in May next." The company was harvesting shingles in a "much larger quantity" than ever before, with more than 1,478,540 three- and two-footers "already received and paid for" since May 15 and "large counts still to come in." More than 1,200,000 shingles had been sold. Adding to the good news, the Riddicks had agreed to pay $371 for the shingles their crews had taken on the disputed lands along Lake Drummond. Finally, Hall had approved the construction of three new lighters to facilitate transportation of shingles produced at the lake.[23]

On January 18, 1817, Hall reported that he had opened the new shingling season by contracting with Swepson to operate lighters along the canal and with James Holladay to cart shingles from the lake camp to the canal. Hall predicted that the 1817 shingling season would require "upwards of a hundred shingle gitters" who would produce nearly three million three-foot shingles and a smaller number of two foot shingles.[24] Two months later, Hall explained that recent winter weather had caused delays in obtaining some items of equipment since "the hands will not agree to get them yet," indicating that the enslaved laborers in his charge had at least some ability to set the terms of their labor. Hall was also continuing his efforts to chase "intruders" away from the disputed area near the lake.[25]

By April, according to Hall, "at least one hundred shingle giters" were at work, and improvements had been made to the cart roads, which Holladay's crews had begun to use. However, "the price of shingles will not keep at $18" and might fall as low as $15.00 per load. Despite the Dismal's isolation, its shingle camps were connected to mid-Atlantic markets, and the market price in Philadelphia had declined to twenty dollars. And even though revenues were slumping, the swamp's canals needed maintenance, which would require an additional "8 to 10 hands." Hall was actively looking for laborers and had hopes that "Mr. Swepson will share his for the purpose," but extra incentives might be needed: Swepson might have to "make their wages equal to what they would earn by giting shingles."[26] Once again, enslaved laborers had some power to dictate the terms of their employment. That Hall reported at least one hundred getters in the DSC land tract in April 1817 constitutes evidence of a significant number of enslaved laborers in the swamp.

At the end of June Hall noted that a group of speculators, Arthur and Lemuel Butt, had dispatched laborers to a tract adjoining the DSC claim and that the Riddicks had dispatched a group of enslaved laborers to protect their claim against the Butts. Hall also advised that it would be "prudent to continue some hands close" to the disputed boundary with the Riddicks. Hall had begun to pay the enslaved lakeside shingle getters four dollars per load (wages later conveyed to their enslavers) but reported that they included "no more than thirty hands at present" and advised his superiors to send more.[27] Six weeks later, Hall had been busy visiting various sectors of the swamp and found "many gitters" at work. In addition, he had employed "from 18 to 20 hands to put the timber in the canal after it is got & float it down."[28]

When the shingling season ended in November 1817, Hall informed Henderson that three-foot shingles were selling at fifteen dollars per thousand and that the DSC's enslaved crews had produced a large number "considering the quantity of hands employed in the giting of them." Hall estimated that the Riddicks' illicit camp had produced nearly one hundred thousand three-foot shingles. The enslaved laborers there had run a road to within sixty yards of the DSC line and then crossed over to cut timber up to three hundred yards into the company's claim. Hall believed that Josiah Riddick was unaware of the trespass but had no doubt that Mills Riddick "carries on the business," despite his denials.[29]

As the 1818 shingling season opened, the DSC managers decided to fight the Riddicks' ongoing trespassing by filing a suit in the Superior Court of Nansemond County, where they owned property. The managers also sued the Riddicks for breach of contract after they failed to complete a canal. In addition, the managers had sold canal stock for $220 per share, raising $5,500 that they directed Hall to use to purchase enslaved people, though he was to spend no more than $600 per person. Hall bought three "fellows" under age twenty-four, paying $450 for one and $500 for each of the others. He was considering two others, for whom he would pay no more than $500 apiece if they were "likely and young."[30]

Hall then turned to areas where the news was less good. Winter weather had hindered Swepson's efforts to survey and cut timber for a mill. Hall had also had no success in finding a vessel to transport twenty thousand two-foot shingles from Suffolk to Alexandria for less than three dollars per thousand, a cost Hall judged too expensive. Further, Hall reported, "I have stated to the shingle gitters that I shall not give this year more than $3 per thousand for gitting, but I am informed that they will give $4 at deep Creek if so they will get all the good shingle gitters from us." Hall closed his letter on a more upbeat note: he had contracted to pay Holladay two dollars per thousand for carting and one dollar per thousand for lightering three-foot shingles.[31]

On March 10, Hall reported having spent $450 to purchase another enslaved laborer, bringing the company's total to four. Hall was still seeking to buy two more and had attended a Suffolk auction but judged the prices to be too high—$690 for each man or boy. The shingling season had begun as Hall had ordered carts and enslaved shingle getters into the swamp, and he had reiterated to the enslaved shinglers that he would pay no more than three dollars per thousand for three-foot shingles, though he continued to worry that the Deep Creek outfit was paying a dollar more. Hall had sent "all the companys hands" to the lake to repair the cart roads, clear the company's canal to the lake, and shore up the towpath.[32]

Ten days later, Hall reported that a snowstorm would hinder the shingling effort for almost two more weeks. However, carts and horses were already at the lake, and once the weather warmed, Hall and Holladay would oversee "a very good years work." Vessels had finally arrived in Suffolk, and Hall had sold shingles for fifteen dollars per thousand.[33]

On August 29, Hall reported that the DSC's canal had been low for most of the spring and early summer, but Hall hoped that late summer rains would elevate the water levels so that a "good years work" in shingles might yet take place. Shingles remained at fifteen dollars in Suffolk, though he had recently held a reserve stock for nearly two weeks in the effort to sell at sixteen dollars. The lack of rain also meant that the grain mill at Jericho was operating at only enough capacity to grind for two or three neighbors "and the swamp hands."[34]

When Hall wrote in late October 1818, he had met with Josiah Riddick to discuss the possibility that the DSC would purchase the Riddicks' old plantation, but Riddick was not amenable to the company's offer. John Bartee had taken over Robert Butt's shingling operation and was floating shingles down the company's canal; Hall had told Bartee's shinglers that if they encroached on company lands, he would end their access to the canal. Though no trespass had yet occurred, Hall was checking on the line at least once a month. In an unusual note, Hall mentioned one of Bartee's enslaved shinglers by name: the agent was keeping "a sharp eye" on "Old Culpepper," who was "working a longside the companys line and will git over if he has a chance of it." The abnormally dry summer had limited shingling operations, resulting in slight decrease in production and sales, although the price had risen slightly to $15.50. And Holladay had declined to continue carting and lightering shingles for the company.[35]

In his December 8 update, Hall explained that the dry weather had persisted into the fall, limiting the size of the loads that could be lightered down the canal. Swamp undergrowth—or perhaps renegade shinglers or maroons—had obscured some of the DSC's survey lines, and two attempts to resurvey them had failed: Hall had concluded that the line would need to be redrawn according to the plat, which was in Henderson's possession. To replace Holladay, Hall was negotiating with John G. Cahoon.[36]

But Hall did not know that as he wrote that letter, James Henderson was already dead. Thomas Griffin informed the agent of the company president's passing in a December 4 letter, to which Hall responded on December 28. Hall summarized the summer shingling season for Griffin's benefit and provided some additional information: the company's enslaved shingle crew amounted to "a bout 50 hands this year." Hall requested that Griffin "please advise me how the business shall be carried on the next year, how many Hands shall be employed in giting of shingles and what I shall give for the cartage of them."[37]

On January 22, 1819, Hall reported that he had persuaded Holladay to reconsider his refusal to cart and lighter shingles and that he had now agreed to do so for the upcoming season. Hall was planning to hire "all the good shingle gitters" he could find, though the outfit at Deep Creek continued to entice enslavers to hire out their men there.[38] In late February, Hall explained his plan for the 1819 shingling season. Weather permitting, Holladay would send twelve to fourteen horses and carts into the swamp around March 1, with five or six more horses and carts following two weeks later, thereby putting the company's operations at the capacity the shingle roads could handle.[39]

The 1819 season was not a particularly good one for the DSC, with fewer than 835,000 three-foot shingles sold for prices no higher than $15.00 per thousand and some as low as $13.50. And Hall anticipated that market prices would continue to fall. Nevertheless, Hall remained confident that the cost of hiring shingle getters would not exceed three dollars per thousand for the next season. Holladay had again declined a new contract for carting and lightering, so Hall recommended that Griffin search for a new contractor. Hall also reported Thomas Swepson's death on October 19.[40]

Only two letters written by Hall during 1820 have survived. In April, Hall reported not only that the price for shingles had fallen to $12.50 per thousand but also that the vessels that had called at Suffolk did not have money on hand to purchase the shingles. Hall had consequently decided not to ship shingles on consignment. Though the dry spell had finally subsided, the company now faced the opposite problem: recent rains had been so heavy that the swamp's water table was unseasonably high, meaning that the shingle getters were "hardly able to do any thing."[41] At the end of June, Hall declared that operations were proceeding "as well as possible." Hall oversaw "from thirty to fourty hands a giting of shingles," and Holladay was again responsible for carting and lightering shingles. Prices remained low—$12.50 per thousand.[42]

By 1820, Frederick Hall had become a capable DSC agent. In addition to managing the company's shingle production, Hall also oversaw the operation of the gristmill at Jericho. Though it failed to produce sufficient quantities for the company to sell, it did provide enough to sustain the DSC's enslaved laborers—thirty-six barrels of corn in the first five months of 1820.[43] And though Hall did not mention them by name, managing the company's enslaved laborers comprised a significant portion of his responsibilities. His letters thus add texture to our understanding of the Dismal's extractive and informal slave economies.

Prior to 1815, the story of the Dismal Swamp is the story of a remote landscape in which maroons moved about with little interaction with whites as land and canal companies gradually increased their incursions. At that point, however, the DSC and DSCC had made significant inroads and firmly established themselves. By the early 1820s, the DSC constituted a robust enterprise that regularly dispatched agents, supplies, and enslaved people into the swamp to protect the company's interests there and to generate profits for shareholders.

The company's growth resulted in an increasingly voluminous paper trail, which, in turn, featured increasing detail regarding the operations of the DSC's slave labor camps. Subsistence supplies for canal cutters included salt, rice, corn, pears, sugar, pork, bacon, spirits, and tobacco. Other supplies included clothing, material, and blankets. Enslaved laborers received these supplies at canal and shingle sites and subsequently traded the goods to maroons deeper in the swamp. These enterprises fused together enslaved shinglers, company agents, and company shareholders in networks of exchange that were clandestine only in that they remained local knowledge before the 1830s and informal only in that they were not sanctioned by the county and state governments of Virginia and North Carolina.

As Moses Grandy labored to earn his freedom for the third time, Nathaniel Turner, enslaved in Southampton County, moved about the Virginia Southside, preaching in secret to enslaved audiences. In 1830, increasingly frustrated by his situation, Turner organized a revolt against the county's enslavers. The August 1831 Southampton Rebellion resulted in the deaths of as many as sixty whites, raising alarm in Virginia and beyond.

rebellion

CHAPTER 5

"Intention of the Negroes Was to Reach the Dismal Swamp"

The Turner Rebellion, Rising Abolition, and the Dismal's Slave Labor Camps

On August 29, 1831, the reading public in Washington, D.C., awoke to reports of unrest in the Virginia Southside over the previous several days. According to the information published in the *Daily National Intelligencer*, "a number of negros, chiefly runaways, combined on Sunday, for the purpose of plunder." The initial marauding bands, led by Nathaniel Turner, had "committed some murders" before more enslaved rebels proceeded to the county courthouse in Jerusalem. Just outside of town, the rebels met a small force of hastily mustered militia, whose members quickly stopped the rebels' advance and then, joined by reinforcements, retaliated with a campaign of terror against enslaved people, "scour[ing] the country and secur[ing] all the misguided wretches who have taken part in this insurrection." "In all the affairs," the *Intelligencer*'s editor observed, "the whites have not lost a man," and he concluded that there existed "no cause for the slightest alarm."[1]

But the *Intelligencer* also reported that some rebels had not yet been rounded up and were believed to be "seeking shelter in the swamps"—the Great Dismal, more than twenty miles to the east of Jerusalem. The *Intelligencer* also quoted a letter written in Greeneville County, to the west of Southampton, in which the author alleged that the "intention of the negroes was to reach the Dismal swamp." The *Richmond Constitutional Whig*, too, reported that several co-conspirators were "dodging about in the swamps, in parties of three and four."[2]

Virginia whites thus saw the Great Dismal as offering the rebels a refuge from local militia. As fears of a massive slave rebellion grew throughout the American Southeast, rumors began to spread that other slaves in northeastern North Carolina had been plotting to join Turner, echoing the reports that had arisen in the wake of Gabriel's conspiracy and the Easter conspiracies three decades earlier. The rumors reflected local fears of petit marronage. Dismal Swamp Land Company (DSLC) and Dismal Swamp Canal Company (DSCC) shareholders had extra reasons to hope that the rebellion would be quickly quashed, as the presence of rebels in the swamp would threaten their ability to make profits there.

According to attorney Thomas R. Gray's transcription of Turner's account, Turner explained that he and his band of rebels traveled a circuitous but purposeful route through Southampton County on August 21 and 22, stopping at sixteen predesignated houses and executing twelve white men, nineteen white women, and twenty-four white children. The rebels' advance on the county courthouse was stopped near Jerusalem, and local militias subsequently killed forty-two slaves and two free black men. Turner fled the skirmish and went into hiding in the woods on the night of August 23, a short walk from the house where his enslaver, Joseph Travis, lay slain.

The next day, Turner observed in the distance a company of white men in search of rebels who remained in flight, and on August 25, he moved to a more secluded hideout under a pile of fence rails in a field a mile to the west of the old plantation, where he had been born. Turner remained secluded there through September and into October. On October 15, a slave, Red Nelson, sighted Turner, and on October 27, Nathaniel Francis observed the fugitive emerging from his den. Francis fired a shot that passed through Turner's hat, but Turner fled. Three days later, a party of fifty men with dogs began searching the area. Armed with a shotgun, Benjamin Phipps encountered Turner, who surrendered.[3]

On October 31, a procession carried Turner through St. Luke's Parish to the courthouse at Jerusalem, where magistrates James Trezvant and James W. Parker and attorney William C. Parker interrogated Turner for two and a half hours, though his attorney, Gray, was not present. Turner later said that he had witnessed nearly fifteen slayings, was party to at least three, and claimed sole responsibility for one.[4] Unlike the conspiracies of 1800 and 1802, the rebellion had originated entirely within St. Luke's Parish and was planned solely by Turner.[5] St. Luke's Parish resident John Boykin testified that Turner attributed his actions to a divine impulse he had felt as early as 1826.[6] Turner was tried on November 5, convicted, and hanged on No-

The Discovery of Nat Turner.

The Discovery of Nat Turner, from E. Benjamin Andrews, *History of the United States, from the Earliest Discovery of America to the End of 1902* (New York: Scribner's, 1903–12). Schomburg Center for Research in Black Culture, Jean Blackwell Hutson Research and Reference Division, New York Public Library Digital Collections, http://digitalcollections.nypl.org/items/510d47df-a10b-a3d9-e040-e00a18064a9.

vember 11. His body was then drawn and quartered, and local whites, eager
to desecrate Turner's remains, claimed souvenirs, including Turner's skull.

    Historians and scholars have chronicled the ways that the brutal repri-
sals against Turner, his conspirators, and free blacks in Southampton fore-
shadowed the hardened racial divisions that undergirded slavery in antebellum Virginia and North Carolina.[7] In the wake of the Southampton
Rebellion, the burden of documenting the Dismal's enslaved laborers shifted
from local land and canal companies to county clerks, who began keeping
detailed registries. From this vantage point, it is perhaps surprising that DSLC
and DSCC officials remained more focused on white land speculators and
market demand for products than on the threat that enslaved people would
use the Dismal as a refuge from which to plot insurrection.
    As in other eras, the surviving documentation provides information re-
garding how company slaves functioned in the Dismal and how they resisted the worst conditions of swamp slavery. The fears that the rebels would
reach the Dismal show that the swamp had already become crystallized in
enslavers' collective imagination as a magnet for enslaved people engaged
in petit marronage. Circumstances in the slave labor camps were such that
slaves already possessed some power to resist collectively, negotiating the
pace and conditions of their forced labors. Turner's rebellion provided many
Virginians and North Carolinians with further evidence that enslaved people constituted an internal enemy, threatening not just slaveholders' finances
but also their lives.
    As historian Manisha Sinha has argued, slave resistance, along with black
activism, formed the core of the rising abolitionist movement.[8] Coupled
with petit marronage, that resistance also provided Virginians and North
Carolinians with more than enough reason to redouble their efforts to
strengthen slave societies locally, regionally, and nationally. During the antebellum era, Virginia men of both prominent national political parties, the
Whigs and Democrats, defended slavery against abolitionists' criticisms and
portrayed abolitionists as enemies of the commonwealth and of the wider
American South.[9] An antislavery bloc of western Virginians grew in influence, demanding political rights equal to those of slaveholding elites from
tidewater counties. But eastern Virginians feared that westerners would seek
to weaken slavery and responded by withholding proportional representa-
tion and universal suffrage for white men. As historian Eva Sheppard Wolf

has explained, by 1832, racial fears formed the impetus for both emancipation and colonization schemes, reflecting a shift from some revolutionary Virginians' antislavery concerns to a more conservative focus on protecting the rights of white men.[10] In North Carolina, too, the General Assembly had severely restricted manumission by the 1830s. Emancipation required an enslaver to post a $1,000 bond guaranteeing that the newly freed person would leave the state within ninety days. Those who remained beyond that time could be "taken up" by a county sheriff and sold back into slavery, as could anyone who returned to the state even briefly to visit family.[11]

But despite the growing fears of slave rebellion and the changes that they provoked, patterns of slave labor and petit marronage in the Great Dismal appear not to have altered considerably. Virginia slaveholder, agriculturalist, and southern nationalist Edmund Ruffin visited the Great Dismal in November 1836. There he saw a camp occupied by a pair of enslaved shingle getters who sheltered in a shanty and learned that such habitations were typical; shanties might shelter as many as six people, with roofs no more than four feet off the ground and sloped to one side to permit rainwater to drain. Shinglers bedded down on the wood shavings produced when making shingles. A slaveholder himself, Ruffin opined that the Dismal's shingle getters "live plentifully and are pleased with their employment—and the main objection to it with their masters, (they being generally slaves,) and the community, is that the laborers have too much leisure time." According to Ruffin, the five hundred or so enslaved shinglers employed by the DSLC performed "heavy labors" that "generally finished in five, and often in four days," after which they spent the "remainder of the week" out of the swamp "given to idleness, and many to drunkenness."[12]

Despite such supposedly idle and drunken workers, the DSLC was thriving, with its stock selling at more than fifteen thousand dollars and returning strong dividends by the 1830s. During the first half of the decade, the company's Suffolk agent was William Shepherd, who continued his predecessors' responsibilities—protecting the DSLC's claims from locals who disputed survey lines; facilitating the purchase and distribution of food and clothing to swamp camps; hiring enslaved laborers from local slaveholders; and drafting regular reports regarding the business. His successor, Joseph Holladay, did the same.

In December 1832, Shepherd exchanged letters with Josiah Riddick that would have been familiar to his predecessors: Riddick and several of his kin were continuing to claim swamp acreage that the company believed was part of its original forty-thousand-acre claim. After detailing exactly what

they're secluded → power comes from hope, they have none

land the Riddicks believed was theirs, Josiah declared that he did not wish to claim land or cut trees that were not legally his.[13] In response, Shepherd outlined the DSLC's competing claim and insisted that no determinations could be made before the "Proprietors of land" affirmed their deeds or grants. Shepherd also argued that Riddick's conception of the lines was "intirely mistaken" and cited a survey conducted by Thomas Draper to back up this assertion. Shepherd noted "that it is my duty as an agent to stop anyone from culling timbers over the supposed lines of the Company" and echoed previous DSLC agents by offering to have the tract resurveyed at the company's expense.[14]

In October 1833, Shepherd recorded purchases of key provisions for the DSLC's swamp camps from two separate merchants. He paid $123.37 of the company's money to Norfolk merchants Kyle and Paul for four sets of blue kersey, three sets of gray kersey, six cotton osnaburgs, one spool of blue thread, and gray and black pilot buttons. At the bottom of the bill, the merchants noted that their "entire winter stock" was already on hand and that they would happily sell to the company "on the best terms such articles as you think proper."[15] And over the summer 1833 shingling season, Shepherd purchased $4.89 worth of supplies from Jesse Perry: three salt sacks, two bottles of ink, one packet of paper, rice, sugar, and two loads of pork and a load of bacon that were sent to the canal camp.[16] In 1835, Shepherd reported having spent $6.00 on twenty-six pairs of socks for enslaved laborers cutting the canal as well as $252.50 for several deliveries of corn, $145.25 for pork, and $16.61 for cotton osnaburgs.[17]

By 1834, Shepherd was drafting monthly standardized reports that apprised DSLC president Robert Butler of shingle loads and sales, listing debits, credits, debts, and debtors. Shepherd also provided context regarding swamp operations as well as information regarding other would-be swamp speculators who contacted him. In February 1834, Shepherd told his boss that although the swamp was so wet that only two lighters were in operation, he had sold some three-foot shingles at twenty dollars per load and two-footers at twelve dollars per load.[18] In March, the captain of a vessel that called at the Suffolk port refused to buy any shingles because their price had fallen in Philadelphia.[19] Another captain returned from Philadelphia in April 1834 and provided a similarly "gloomy account of the market." Moreover, Shepherd "was in the swamp last Thursday & the b[ul]k of the canal was from ankle to half leg" deep, meaning that lighters could not pass through.[20] The depressed prices for shingles continued into the fall, when despite the return of rains that filled the swamp's waterways, "nothing shows more plainly the failure of good timber than the reduced stock with diminished sales to those of last year."[21] These problems persisted through 1835 as well.[22] Such conditions required Shepherd to carefully manage the enslaved people on whom the DSLC depended to cut shingles. In December 1833, he mentioned that he had hired enslaved shinglers for the upcoming season at the same prices he had paid in January 1833.[23] In May 1835, Shepherd advised the DSLC that at least two company slaves had "gone over the sound in Washington Co. N.C.," apparently having been enticed "by the fine tales of some of those who" were compelled to labor as slaves at Somerset Place, North Carolina's largest antebellum plantation.[24]

Between 1833 and 1835, William Shepherd hired a number of enslaved people from local slaveholders, signing annual contracts on the DSLC's behalf. These contracts provide the first substantive evidence regarding the terms by which the DSLC hired slaves. Shepherd's contracts generally began on New Year's Day, made no reference to workers' surnames or physical appearance, and often referred to the enslaved shinglers as "boys." A standard provision of the contracts called for the DSLC to provide each hired slave with "good clothing and a hat." For example, on January 1, 1833, Shepherd promised to pay Sewellin Jones sixty dollars "for the Hire of boys Fabin and Randall for the use of the Dismal Swamp Land Co."[25] On January 1, 1835, Shepherd signed four contracts, among them one with Jones, from whom he hired three enslaved people—Fabin, Randall, and Henry—at a cost of one hundred dollars.[26] One of the 1835 contracts involved Lemuel Holland, to whom the DSLC would pay sixty-five dollars "for the hire of Jacob & Michael."[27] Another contract obligated Shepherd to pay Jacob Keeling (Holland's assignee) ninety dollars "for the hire of boys Nat, Max, and Anthony."[28] The fourth contract provided more detail than the others. The contract stipulated that before Christmas 1835, Shepherd would "*pay* or *cause* to be paid unto John S. Denson or his assign, the Just and full Sum of *Thirty* dollars and _____ cents, current money of Virginia" to hire George. In addition, Shepherd promised to provide George "*with two* suits of good *clothes*, two *pairs shoes*, stockings, Hat, and blanket." And finally, Shepherd promised that George would "*be* returned" to Denson by Christmas Day.[29]

The parties to the contracts went to some effort to ensure that enslaved persons were provisioned during their time under the control of the DSLC. For the DSLC, such contracts encoded crucial protections against charges of maltreatment that an enslaver might bring in court. However, such contractual provisions also offer a reminder of the particularly dangerous nature of swamp slavery. Enslaved shingle getters and canal porters were subject to illness caused by working in extreme heat and humidity, transmitted by mosquitoes and flies, or as a result of snakebites. Company slaves were also subject to injuries caused by pickaxes, saws, or other tools of the trade.

Slave hire contracts of course contain no indicators of these men's thoughts regarding their circumstances. As in other extant records, these men's presence is reduced to several lines that emphasize the primacy of the currency that exchanged hands between DSLC agents and local slaveholders. But by providing contractual provisions against maltreatment and for food and clothing, the DSLC ensured that it had a steady supply of the slave labor it required to maintain its business. And in so doing, they enable us to learn about the items that enslaved laborers exchanged with the Dismal's maroons.

By late 1835, Joseph Holladay had replaced Shepherd as the DSLC's Suffolk agent. Holladay's quarterly and monthly reports to the DSLC shareholders regularly listed food provisions and extended discussions of the ebbs and flows in the production of shingles and staves.[30] In February 1836, Holladay explained to Butler that rains had rendered the swamp unusually wet, making entry impossible, bringing company business to a halt, and likely reducing interactions between maroons in the swamp's depths and the DSLC's agents and enslaved canal cutters.[31] Three months later, Holladay reported further problems: after spending three days surveying timber on lands claimed by a speculator, shingle getters declared that what existed did not warrant the expense of constructing an access road. However, Holladay apparently believed that the enslaved shingle getters had an illicit arrangement with the speculator: the agent suggested that Butler secure a warrant empowering the company to bring the shingle getters before a magistrate, who would likely order a public whipping as punishment for working in the speculator's employ on DSLC lands.[32]

On June 30, Holladay reported that unseasonably dry weather had resulted in an insufficient amount of timber, "although there are as many hands in the swamp as I would wish." The laborers ultimately "quit their work," some compelled to harvesting wheat on local farms, some "looking for other imployment." But Holladay seemed less concerned about shingle getters dispersing around the region than about the effects of the paucity of timber on the site's annual yield.[33] In October 1836, Holladay recorded receipts for ten yards of cotton cloth for $8.75 and drab kersey intended for swamp laborers at a cost of $16.12.[34]

In 1837, the DSLC's location did not insulate it from the shock waves that spread outward from the crisis in the banking sectors of New Orleans, New York City, and England.[35] Holladay struggled to facilitate sales of company timber throughout the year, but in the spring of 1838, finally able to sell some shingles, he began to take a more optimistic tone.[36] In May 1838, Holladay's second-quarter report further brightened the outlook, noting an increased demand for the swamp's lumber along with an uptick in sales. Many more "hands [were] ingaged in geting lumber than were this time last year." By June, the demand for shingles exceeded what he could supply, and the company was seeking additional enslaved shingle getters just as hot weather and voracious flies were making the work particularly onerous. The optimism persisted through the first quarter of 1839, when Holladay anticipated "20 or more hands in the swamp this year than the preceding year."[37]

The extant documents suggest that the DSLC continued to hire enslaved people from local slaveholders, though those slaveholders changed over time. In what might have been Holladay's first act after assuming his post was to inform Butler that Nat, Max, and Anthony had been hired under an annual contract with Keeling at a cost of $110. In addition to these holdovers, Holladay contracted with a man named Harrell to pay thirty dollars for the annual hire of Allen, who was "to have the usual winter and summer clothing, and a blanket."[38] Between December 27, 1844, and January 1, 1848, Holladay signed five slave hire contracts on behalf of the DSLC. For Anthony, Holladay paid $20.25 to Robert Rogers. For Edward and Elijah, Holladay paid $40.00 to John C. Cahoon. For Selvy, Holladay paid $25.00 to Elisha Norfleet. For Littleton, Holladay paid $25.00 to Caty Copeland. And for Bob and Edmon, Holladay paid $102.00 to Henry Rawls. In all of the agreements except the one with Rawls, Holladay promised to provide each slave with clothing, a hat, and a blanket; Bob and Edmon received only "good customary clothing."[39] There is no evidence that any of these men were able to use the wages paid to their owners to purchase freedom.

Although Nat Turner's rebellion had little effect on the daily operations of the DSLC or on the enslaved men who labored on its behalf, tangible evidence of the fears inspired by the revolt can be seen in from the laws it inspired. Beginning in the 1830s, land companies were required to register enslaved people who labored in the Dismal's canal and timber camps. Aimed not only at regulating the movements of Virginians and North Carolinians who fled enslavement, these laws also sought to dictate how whites who lived on the fringes of the two states' slave societies would engage the swamp's enslaved laborers. Enslaved canal and timber laborers often bore the scars of swamp toil, and the county clerks recorded those scars, in the process creating a record of slavery's continued oppression of enslaved blacks in the Lower Chesapeake. The absence of references to overt slave resistance in the surviving documentation does not mean that these people were docile or accepted their fate. The subsistence goods that Shepherd and Holladay sent into the swamp's slave labor camps—cloth, socks, salt, rice, sugar, pork, and corn—offer strong evidence of the area's informal slave economy.

By the 1840s, the DSLC's efforts to wring profit out of the Dismal took place against a backdrop of significant economic change, as the great Chesapeake tobacco plantations had already faded largely away. In their stead, Virginia planters broadened their agricultural enterprises to include new tobacco-planting regions in the piedmont and grain and pork enterprises on what had once been tobacco land. These changes reduced the number of large plantations with slave populations that numbered in the hundreds, resulting in a variety of proposals for ways to reduce the size of the commonwealth's enslaved population. Though a small number of Virginians granted manumission papers to the enslaved, leading to a significant rise in the state's free black population, most slaveholders sought further financial gain by selling enslaved people to traders who supplied the new slave markets in the Southwest or to remove former slaves entirely from the United States via colonization in West Africa. Still other Virginians sought local markets for their enslaved laborers, and the DSLC became the region's primary hirer. It was in this context that the Great Dismal Swamp attracted the attention of black abolitionists and their allies beginning in the 1840s. And the most prominent of these abolitionists was Frederick Douglass, a fugitive slave who became a noted newspaper editor, intellectual, and lecturer.

CHAPTER 6

"Slaves in the Dismal Swamp"

Abolitionists and the Dismal's
Extractive Economy of Slavery

In 1848, Frederick Douglass's *North Star* reprinted a report, "Slaves in the Dismal Swamp," that had originally appeared in the *Zion's Herald*, a weekly magazine published in Boston from 1823 to 1828. The Great Dismal Swamp was worthy of notice because it harbored a "city of refuge" for "the poor slave." "Hundreds of fugitives" populated the swamp's "asylum from oppression" in a land so inaccessible that many had "never seen a white man." To sustain themselves, the Dismal's fugitive rebels bartered with "slaves who have their tasks in parts of the swamp." In contrast to the fugitives, the "faithful" enslaved laborers produced shingles in exchange for rations granted every two weeks. Food rations included "a barrel of pork and two barrels of flour." Through this arrangement, enslaved people facilitated an informal economy that supported fugitives marooned in remote swamp sectors.[1]

At the time of the report, however, the fugitive camp had become less secure. A local informant who witnessed a skirmish between a party of slave hunters with dogs and the maroons armed with guns told *Zion's Herald* that the hunters had used long guns to shoot four of the absconders "down like partridges"; several others had been wounded and unable to escape. The piece ended with a query: "If the slaves were happy in their present condition, would they prefer a residence in the Dismal Swamp to it?"[2] Even before Moses Grandy arrived in Boston to share his firsthand account of

marronage in the Dismal, and a generation before Edmund Jackson characterized the Dismal's fugitive slaves as "the Virginia Maroons," then, the editors of *Zion's Herald* had sought to disseminate the story of the Dismal's informal economy of exchange, its rumors of slave flight and marronage, its
context for enslaved shinglers and canal cutters.

Plumbing this story's depths requires highlighting the broader contexts of
abolitionist agitations and slave resistance in the antebellum United States.
Modern sensibilities might compel us to respond negatively to the writer's
question. Frequently considered "dismal" for its lack of neat roads, antebellum dwellings, and British or American manufactured goods that reflected
the growing consumer power of the new middle class in the early American republic, the swamp was not yet a settled landscape.[3] A few white Virginians saw the potential to provide travelers or vacationers with lodging on
Lake Drummond's shores.[4] Other members of the area's elite, particularly
canal and land company officials who rarely visited the swamp, saw its trees
as its most valuable resource. Regular visits to the swamp's slave labor camps
provided company agents—but not company officials—with direct knowledge of the Dismal's semipermanent residents, the hundreds of shingle getters, canal cutters, and timber carters who were compelled to produce goods
for the region's extractive economy in the service of Atlantic markets. Seeking personal and company financial gain, agents often turned a blind eye
while slaves engaged the Dismal's maroons in informal economies of exchange. For the poorer and middling white Virginians and North Carolinians who worked as agents—the Jacob Collees, Thomas Shepherds, Thomas
Swepsons, and Samuel Proctors—tacit acceptance of informal slave economies of exchange and petit marronage sustained their families and perhaps
even permitted a rise in society. In many cases, these men and others placed
a premium on negotiations with and accommodation of the Dismal's enslaved laborers.

What did the *Zion's Herald* writer seek to imply when he referred to the
fugitive slaves' "present condition"? What implicit meanings did his reference to a Dismal Swamp "residence" hold? The *North Star*'s readers undoubt-
edly sensed the irony implicit in the *Zion's Herald* writer's question. Those
readers might call into question the widely articulated tropes of southern
slavery that by 1848 had come to shape the narrative of unfreedom and its
spread into the Cotton Kingdom: orderly plantations, docile slaves, benevo-
lent masters who held important rank as social and political elites in southern slave societies. Douglass's readers might now add to these tropes the

Great Dismal's context for an extractive economy of slavery, at least a generation old, complete with an informal economy of exchange.

Dating to the 1820s, the calls for the immediate abolition of slavery gained traction among a strand of predominantly black abolitionists who were emboldened by British and American bans on the transatlantic slave trade and enraged by southern intransigence and the growing domestic slave trade. In the context of growing racial inequality and disfranchisement in the North, black abolitionists called for an immediate end to slavery and pointed to white politicians' collective failure to uphold the doctrine of equality inherent in the U.S. Constitution. Immediate abolitionists operated along two trajectories, at times intersecting and at times divergent: the intersection of broader reform efforts that highlighted slavery's immoralities and that had been informed by eighteenth-century British antislavery strategies; and the more recent tradition of black protest, argued most eloquently by David Walker's excoriating critique of American republican government in his appeal to American blacks.[5]

As slavery became more deeply entrenched in the United States, state legislatures moved to close all avenues for black enfranchisement.[6] In 1835, North Carolina legislators banned the state's small population of free blacks from voting for members of the General Assembly.[7] In 1836, so many antislavery petitions had flooded Congress that the U.S. House of Representatives prohibited discussion of the subject on the House floor until 1844. A number of southern states responded to abolitionist agitation by outlawing the distribution of antislavery pamphlets under penalty of fines or imprisonment, particularly targeting black seamen who crewed vessels that called at southern ports, fearful that these sailors carried with them incendiary antislavery literature. The proslavery coalition of Whigs and Democrats that upheld the gag rule on discussion of antislavery legislation reflected the deepening entrenchment of slaveholding interests at the federal level.[8]

Abolitionists responded to this rising federal Slave Power in a number of ways. In 1840, the members of the American Anti-Slavery Society, led by William Lloyd Garrison, decided to abstain from voting, turning instead to strategies aimed at shaping a national "moral cordon" of public opinion that would isolate slavery's supporters: holding public meetings, distributing antislavery literature and petitions, and supporting public antislavery lectures.

Other abolitionists organized alternative antislavery political parties, including the Liberty Party and the Free Soil Party. "Free soil, free labor" became a particular rallying cry articulated by antislavery northerners who sought to defend the moral and economic superiority of northern societies by contrast to southern locales they described as yoked to slave labor. As historian Eric Foner has observed, the dichotomous public discourse around free labor obscured the fact that "free labor" implied "two distinct economic conditions": one in which wage laborers sought employment in the marketplace and another in which smaller landholders in a broader range of locations struggled to maintain economic independence in an Atlantic context of global economic exchange.[9] Other historians, most recently Christy Clark-Pujara and Joanne Pope Melish, have pointed to the myriad strategies by which northern whites, particularly in New England, sought to compel the removal of blacks from northern towns and, in turn, to propagate the myth that obscured the long legacy of slavery and racial discord in the region's history.[10]

After 1840, slave flight into the Dismal became a major problem for Virginia and North Carolina officials, particularly as antislavery activists became better organized in their efforts to influence public opinion and to persuade state legislatures and the U.S. Congress to outlaw slavery. In 1846–47, North Carolina legislators enacted a statute promoting the "apprehension of runaway slaves in the great Dismal Swamp" to codify company practices of registering enslaved laborers that dated to the early 1830s.[11] By the time Douglass highlighted the Dismal's context for American slavery in 1848, the question of slavery's expansion into the western territories by way of the annexation of the independent Texas Republic and the subsequent Mexican-American War had helped to cause a significant schism in the American abolition movement. At the center of a rising wing of immediate abolitionism animated by black Americans, Douglass closely observed U.S. aggression against Mexico. He knew that Texas's admission to the Union as a slave state did not portend well for the national effort to enclose the South in a "moral cordon" of liberty and antislavery. Proslavery politicians were determined to perpetuate the peculiar institution. Any hope that the federal government would abolish slavery either gradually or immediately was extinguished when Congress passed Kentucky Whig Henry Clay's Compromise of 1850. Included among the five bills was an act that strengthened the existing federal Fugitive Slave Law, dating to 1793, by compelling officials in northern states to assist southern slave catchers pursuing runaways. For immediate abolitionists, the law was clear evidence that southern slaveholders had the full backing of federal officials. Some northern citizens observed and vigorously protested high-profile incidents in which violence or threatened violence forced fugitives to leave northern cities for Canada, England, and other foreign states.[12]

Almost immediately after the passage of the law, a number of well-known runaways fled for England. Among them were William and Ellen Craft, who had escaped Georgia by having Ellen dress as William's male slaveholder, and Henry "Box" Brown, who had toured New England telling the harrowing story of his escape from Virginia in a box mailed to Philadelphia.[13] In 1854, Anthony Burns's rendition trial caused several days of unrest in Boston. Burns, who had escaped Virginia, was marched to the Boston seaport under the guard of federal troops while abolitionists protested vigorously.[14] Slave renditions in the East and in the Ohio River Valley coincided with skirmishes in the Nebraska and Kansas territories from 1852 to 1856, ultimately leading splintered factions of Free Soilers, Liberty men, Whigs, and moderate Democrats to form the Republican Party.[15] As public protests increased against enforcement of the federal Fugitive Slave Law, the rhetoric around the subject of race and slavery's expansion into the western territories continued to increase. In May 1856, the political protests reached a boiling point when Massachusetts senator Charles Sumner was nearly caned to death by South Carolina congressman Preston Brooks on the U.S. Senate floor.[16]

If the *North Star*'s readers were intrigued by the prospect of maroons in the Dismal in the late 1840s, they might have been curious about the operations of the DSLC, the DSCC, and smaller outfits. In particular, the readers of the *North Star* might have identified with Douglass's effort to emphasize the exploitative relationship these companies fostered as they produced increasing quantities of timber via enslaved laborers toiling in the swamp under shadowy circumstances. This point was a ready-made abolitionist trope, adding heft to broader arguments that the continued expansion of slave labor was in fact detrimental to the future of wage labor. By the 1850s, the Dismal's slave labor camps were documented more carefully than in previous years not only by company agents but also by county clerks in accordance with local laws increasingly aimed at limiting black freedom, such as the 1856 Virginia statute that codified the process by which free blacks might be re-enslaved.[17]

This antebellum story of freedom and unfreedom is reflected in the record of Edmond Boothe's life in Virginia's Nansemond County and North Carolina's Gates County.[18] Information on Boothe derives primarily from an 1847–61 register of Native Americans, enslaved canal cutters, and free laborers in Gates County, in the swamp's southwestern corner. In addition to Boothe, the Gates County register lists the names of forty-five other free blacks registered as hands "employed to work in the Great Dismal Swamp."[19] Documents like the Gates County register reflect the problematic observations of the white men who created such records, officials who likely viewed as inferior to whites the black people whose lives were being recorded. Yet, what do Boothe's changing circumstances reveal about the murky legal and social contexts for slavery and freedom in the Great Dismal Swamp and the Lower Chesapeake? What can and cannot be known about his life and those of other blacks in Southside Virginia and northeastern North Carolina? Boothe first appears in the register as a slave in March 1847 and in February 1852 was listed as a free man working as a swamp laborer for the Orapeake Canal Company. By 1857, however, Boothe was again enslaved.

This trajectory reflects blacks' limited prospects for economic independence in the broader context of regional and national turmoil. On June 11, 1833, little more than two years after the Turner Rebellion and one year following the contentious Virginia Constitutional Convention, the town commissioners of Gatesville, North Carolina, appointed Henry R. Pugh as the board's clerk. His duties included maintaining lists of taxable white men and of taxable enslaved men, including the names of the slaveholders to whom they were bound. Three months later, the board organized several patrol companies and charged them with keeping watch "as much as necessary."[20]

At the beginning of each laboring season, the Gates County registrar entered a detailed description of Boothe's physical characteristics. Listed as "the property of Nathaniel Booth of Nansemond County Virginia," Boothe's designation as property privileged his legal status as enslaved by Nathaniel Boothe before his natural humanity. For at least six years—between 1847 and 1852—Edmond Boothe was sent into the swamp by Nathaniel Boothe's agent at Suffolk, William B. Whitehead, an arrangement with its precedent in Dismal Swamp Land Company operations. Though Edmond Boothe became free in 1852, twenty-two free blacks were registered before him. Another twenty-two new free blacks were recorded during his four years of freedom. Several of these men appeared in the registry in multiple years:

Dick Jones (July 1847 and January 1852), Mills Reed (March 1848 and January 1850), Arkey Milteer (June 1852 and October 1855), Bassett Mackey (July 1854, October 1855, and May 1856), and Jack Anderson (June 1852, May 1853, July 1854, and May 1855).

In 1847, Boothe appeared to be "about forty-five years old, Black good teeth, a little gray tolerable full beard with a scar on the Stomache, about 3 inches long and a scar on the out sid of right Kne about an inch long." Without wearing shoes, Boothe stood about "Five Feet eight & ½ inches high," and he weighed about 176 pounds.[21] Boothe was older than what was typically considered prime age for an enslaved laborer. Boothe's scars likely reflected the dangers of his previous labors or had resulted from an earlier punishment by a slaveholder. Similar entries for Boothe appear at the beginning of the laboring season in over the next few years.

In February 1852, Boothe was no longer enslaved when he presented himself to the Gates County registrar: "Edmond Boothe said to be a free man and hired the present year by William B. Whitehead." Though no longer a slave, Boothe chose to labor in the swamp. The registrar's description noted that Boothe was now "about forty seven years old" and listed his height as five feet, nine inches. He was "stoutly built," with scars on his right hand, on his breast, and below his left eye."[22]

In May 1853, the registrar again reported that Boothe was "said to be a free man." Whitehead had again hired Boothe as "one of his hands." Now "about forty eight years of age" and "of black complexion," Boothe was described in the same terms as the preceding year: "stoutly built, has a scar on his right hand, one on his breast, one on the left side of his face below the eye, and stands without shoes five feet eight inches high."[23]

In July 1854, Boothe appears again in the register, but several significant descriptors set the new entry apart from earlier notations. The Gates County clerk, Henry L. Eure, described Boothe's physical characteristics consistently with previous entries but labeled Edmond as being "of Booth" and as "a free boy of color." Eure noted that Mills Rogers, not William Whitehead, had hired Boothe into the swamp (though Rogers most likely acted as Whitehead's agent).[24] In May 1855, Eure again recorded Boothe as a "free man of color," and his distinguishing physical characteristics had remained constant, though he had aged a year. Whitehead had again hired Boothe into the swamp.[25] In 1856, Boothe was not listed in the Gates County register until September, with no explanation for why he had not entered the swamp earlier in the season, as had been the case in previous years. His physical description remained the same, and his age apparently did not detract from his value to the company as a canal cutter, as long as Boothe was able to perform the arduous labor required of him.[26]

On September 24, 1857, Boothe again appears in the Gates County registry, but on this occasion, he was part of a group entry with "Boys Walker, Albert, Osborn, Sam, Edmond, Jackson, Jeffrey, and Charles" as the "property of Mills Rogers," who had registered them as "his hands employed to work in the Great Dismal Swamp."[27] Though physical descriptions were not included for any of the eight men, a separate document confirms Boothe's identity and explains that he was now "the property of Mills Rogers," who registered Boothe to labor in the Dismal Swamp on behalf of Whitehead. Eure observed Boothe to be of a "dark complexion," noted several scars, and listed his height at about five feet eight inches.[28]

It is not clear why Boothe had returned to enslavement, but historian Tommy Bogger has noted that when enslaved blacks attained freedom in Norfolk, their liberty was tenuous at best.[29] September 1857 constitutes the last time that Edmond Boothe appeared in the register, though he is glimpsed again in an October 1859 request by O. W. Flynn of Suffolk, who sought to dispatch Boothe to labor in the Gates County Dismal Swamp sector.[30] The surviving documentation also does not explain this change in Boothe's circumstances, and other important questions regarding his life of unfreedom similarly remain unanswered. Did Boothe have extended family among Nansemond County's enslaved people? Did he marry and build a family of his own, perhaps explaining his annual returns to the Gates County canal site? Where did he live when not camped in the swamp? Boothe thus offers yet another example of the difficulties that scholars face in reconstructing enslaved peoples' lives. Still, Boothe's story illustrates that at least one enslaved laborer in the Lower Chesapeake transitioned to freedom only to return to swamp slavery.

In 1856, David Hunter Strother visited Horse Camp in the DSLC's sector near Jericho ditch, where he learned that enslaved shingle getters paid maroons for help in bolstering the amount of timber the company's slave labor camps produced. Wanting to see a Virginia maroon, Strother ventured a short distance into the swamp along a canal towpath and encountered the mysterious Osman.[31] Strother's rendition of Osman—a physically imposing, dark-skinned man with thick gray hair, hands gnarled by slave labor, seem-

OSMAN.

Porte Crayon [David Hunter Strother], *Osman the Maroon in the Swamp*, *Harper's New Monthly Magazine*, September 1856. Schomburg Center for Research in Black Culture, Photographs and Prints Division, New York Public Library Digital Collections, http://digitalcollections.nypl.org/items/510d47db-bc35-a3d9-e040-e00a18064a99.

ing to emerge from within the Dismal's thick roots, tangled vines, and hanging Spanish moss—presented a distorted picture of what was by the 1850s a rather customary local economy of exchange set within or near the Dismal's timber and canal camps. Strother's portrait of Osman (fig. 5) captured the paradox of petit marronage and the informal slave economy. This image of an unsettled swamp existence reinforced the lie of benign southern slavery by depicting the dire consequences for those enslaved persons who sought to escape the confines of the system.

DSLC agents had long known of the informal slave economy, and knowledge of it began to leak to broader audiences no later than the 1820s, when the *Zion's Herald* piece appeared. In addition, William Lloyd Garrison printed Henry W. Longfellow's poem, "The Slave in the Dismal Swamp," in the *Liberator* in December 1842.[32] By 1848, Douglass headlined the new generation of black antislavery observers who had begun to write about the Dismal in the effort to bring about immediate emancipation. As slavery's survivors, Douglass, Grandy, Brown, the Crafts, and others, testified to the practical ways that the Slave Power continued to oppress black Americans.[33]

Several novels brought further attention to the Dismal's maroon communities. In 1853, William Wells Brown's *Clotel* placed Nat Turner and several hundred followers in the Dismal. In the same year, Douglass's *The Heroic Slave* told the story of Madison Washington, who hid in a cave in the swamp for five years. In 1859, Martin R. Delany began publishing *Blake; or, The Huts of America*, in which a runaway meets Turner's old followers in the Dismal.[34] And Harriet Beecher Stowe's *Dred: A Tale of the Great Dismal Swamp* was serialized between December 1855 and September 1856, a period that coincided with the most intense fighting between proslavery and antislavery settlers in "Bleeding Kansas."[35] Basing the novel on the various accounts of Turner's retreat to the woods, Stowe tacitly invited her audience undertake a fuller consideration of Turner and other black rebels. *Dred* not only reflected southerners' fears about black uprisings but put forth the possibility that revolt had become the only way that black resistance could end American slavery. Published four years after *Uncle Tom's Cabin*, *Dred* reflected a core shift in Stowe's antislavery ideology: a rejection of West African colonization in the face of the realization that it would not eliminate black resistance. Instead, she believed, nothing short of an end to slavery would suffice.[36]

Stowe based Dred's character on Denmark Vesey, interpreting the reports produced after the Vesey conspiracy to strengthen her implied message that slavery's perpetuation could lead only to large-scale rebellion. But Stowe's characters also reflected her interest in creating a rhetorical link between the leaders of such revolt conspiracies and the Upper South's most famous place of maroon refuge. The Vesey conspiracy had taken place in urban Charleston, South Carolina, where blacks could blend into their own communities for protection but the cityscape offered the advantage to its militia. Though Stowe did not reference the Gabriel or Easter conspiracies, similar circumstances had worked against rebels in Richmond, Norfolk, Petersburg, and other Lower Chesapeake hamlets. Indeed, after Turner's rebellion, the rapid development of urban landscapes and the replacement of haphazard militia by regular patrols were inspired in large part by the threat of slave revolt.

There is no extant documentary evidence that Turner or any of his followers reached the Dismal Swamp. But for abolitionist agitators in the 1850s, the generational history of marronage and slavery in the Great Dismal nonetheless had the potential to illuminate the full scope of slavery's retrenchment in Virginia and North Carolina. For Frederick Douglass, Henry Brown, Anthony Burns, and many more enslaved people who fled Virginia or North Carolina, the Fugitive Slave Law of 1850 clearly demonstrated that enslavers had the support of federal authorities. In this context, other observers, among them landscape architect and journalist Frederick Law Olmsted, were intrigued by the paradoxical form of slavery that undergirded the Dismal Swamp extractive economy. Olmsted cast the story of the swamp's maroons as a recent history of decline, reflecting the many difficulties that company slaves endured and suggesting that the Dismal's maroons maintained only a limited presence in the swamp. Olmsted noted that slave catchers had begun using dogs to track enslaved people, a new strategy that imperiled maroons within the swamp's depths. Olmsted based his claims regarding the depopulation of the swamp on an interview he conducted with Joseph Church, an enslaved Virginian who lived in the area. According to Church, when confronted by slave catchers, some maroons chose death rather than be recaptured. The Dismal's maroons lived in "huts in 'back places' hidden by bushes, and difficult of access," enabling company agents to easily distinguish between maroons and enslaved shingle getters. Church thought that the maroons often appeared scared "and kind o'strange, cause dey hasn't much to eat, and ain't decent like we is." Olmsted saw the maroons as dilapidated, "born outlaws; educated self-stealers" who had been "trained from infancy to be constantly in dread of the approach of a white man as a thing more fearful than wildcats or serpents, or even starvation."[37]

Olmsted's account illustrates that at least one enslaved person identified himself not only in relation to the swamp's slave laborers but also in relation to its maroons. Among Virginians and North Carolinians enslaved in the Lower Chesapeake, these separate levels of self-identification traced to several generations of customs. Unlike the division of slave labor that tightly regulated enslaved peoples' movements on the few remaining large planta-tions in the Virginia tidewater or the tobacco plantations that now popu-lated the Virginia and North Carolina piedmont (though in these contexts, too, enslaved people resisted total control in myriad ways), Dismal Swamp tasks were not overseen through direct oversight on a daily basis, at least be-fore the 1840s. Slavery in the Dismal did bear some resemblance to slavery in urban contexts in that shinglers and canal cutters were able to leverage their skills to obtain the provisions necessary to sustain life at shingle camps. Nevertheless, slavery constrained the lives of the many hundreds of people who labored among the Dismal Swamp's trees, cutting its canals and con-structing its shingle roads. And as a result, abolitionists not only took an in-terest in Dismal Swamp slavery but by the 1850s used marronage to charac-terize the Dismal's context.

Knowledge of the Dismal's maroons attracted much wider abolitionist interest as well, including that of Edmund Jackson. His January 1852 piece on "The Virginia Maroons" described his efforts to determine how long a "colony" of enslaved and free people had lived in the swamp, what portion of this "colony" could be considered "Fugitives" from southern law, and what portion descended from these fugitives. This "city of refuge in the midst of Slavery," he had heard, endured despite its impoverishment relative to the region's landowners and company shareholders. At its core existed a set of "Swamp merchants" whose "entire trade" was with the swamp's "Maroons."[38]

Jackson never claimed to have found this city of refuge but he, like Stowe, had been drawn to the Dismal for its peculiar history of petit marronage.[39] He had already published essays addressing slavery's more widely known ills: the avarice of slaveholders, slave flight as self-emancipation, and the moral, legal, and political debates over the legal status of fugitive runaways that di-vided partisans in both houses of the U.S. Congress. Thus Jackson sought to cast petit marronage not only as a matter of local concern but also as an issue of national intrigue as he called attention to antebellum Boston's contexts of school segregation and racial discrimination. Yet, instead of merely report-ing the existence of slavery at work in the form of swamp labor camps, Jack-son sought to dramatize the institution's ills by characterizing such camps as a "city of refuge." To this end, an awareness of Jackson's efforts to draw atten-tion to the Dismal's maroon encampments adds texture to our understand-ing of black life in the swamp in the generation before the Civil War. In doing so, we learn about the final years during which petit marronage sustained communities in eastern Virginia's and North Carolina's swamplands and of land company officials' and agents' final attempts to turn a blind eye to petit marronage in support of their own swamp ventures.

Heightening production of raw materials, too, accounted for a substantial increase in the number of enslaved laborers in the Great Dismal. When Jackson published his reflections, the Great Dismal had for nearly a century been at the center of various land companies' efforts to improve its swampy soils. These companies operated largely outside of the influence of the rising abolitionist movement, their attentions fixed on serving various markets in the late Atlantic world. In the 1840s, forest industries in the Dismal expanded significantly, substantially increasing the number of enslaved laborers in the swamp and exacerbating the incursions of the industrial nineteenth century into an otherwise remote environment. What had been a vast wetland comprising more than two thousand square miles had been drastically changed by the 1850s, and the chances that the Dismal's maroons would encounter whites increased.

The swamp "community" to which Jackson referred and that inspired *Dred* was not a permanent settlement. Rather, it was comprised of slave labor camps and geographically mobile American maroon groups that had for generations engaged in petit marronage and informal economies of exchange with enslaved laborers. Locals white and black did not offer nonresident observers intricate details regarding how either petit marronage or the informal economies of exchange worked, limiting the historical record regarding these phenomena. Prior to the 1820s, therefore, knowledge of the Great Dismal's context for slave labor remained largely local, and Strother's encounter with Osman in the 1850s likely represents the closest contact between an outsider and a Dismal Swamp maroon. Nevertheless, the accounts of "slaves in the Dismal swamp," if cast rhetorically in broader context, provided Jackson with evidence of a significant maroon "community" with great potential to destabilize the southern slave system. That broader context engaged knowledge of marronage in the Atlantic world: Jamaica, Cuba, Hispaniola, and beyond.

The heritage of resistance and agency in the midst of slavery reflected by petit marronage was sustained until the Civil War. Well after the fighting erupted, the Lower Chesapeake region's major entities, including the Dismal Swamp Land Company and the Dismal Swamp Canal Company, continued to hire slave laborers to maintain the Great Canal and its expanding networks of internal improvements. And the enslaved laborers, in turn, continued to support the maroons who set up camps in the swamp's shrinking remote locations, thus continuing the region's informal economies of exchange. Indeed, Olmsted heard accounts of maroons who could not "obtain the means of supporting life without coming often either to the outskirts to steal from the plantations, or to the neighbourhood of the camps of the lumbermen."[40] Echoing Strother's image of Osman, white Virginians and North Carolinians viewed the Dismal's maroons as strange outsiders, their actions as unlawful pillage, a viewpoint that persisted until after the outbreak of the Civil War.

Abraham Lincoln's November 1860 election to the U.S. presidency proved to be the last straw for the most radical southerners: South Carolina seceded six weeks later. Virginia and North Carolina joined the Confederacy relatively late—in April and May 1861, respectively. As white southerners unified in one last defense of slavery, black Americans moved in droves to Union lines and took up arms to set in motion the elimination of the peculiar institution.[41] Petit marronage in the Great Dismal Swamp likely continued until the passage of the Thirteenth Amendment and the end of American slavery in 1865, when those who had found refuge there could be sure that would not face a return to bondage.

"From Log Cabin to the Pulpit"

*William H. Robinson and the
Late Nineteenth-Century Legacy
of Petit Marronage*

From the early postbellum period into the twentieth century, the legacy of the Dismal's maroons endured. In May 1899, a Salt Lake City newspaper, the *Broad Ax*, denounced recent efforts to "impress the idea upon our mind, that during the existence of slavery in the South there was no friction between the master and the slave." Such a revisionist narrative might not seek to "rekindle the bitter recollections of the past" but nevertheless constituted a "vain effort to prove that slavery was the natural condition of the negro." The Dismal Swamp was home to enslaved shinglers whom company officials had valued at two million dollars, and as a result, "all southerners are familiar with 'the Virginia Maroons.'"[1] In August 1903, the writer, "Correspondent Raymond," submitted an updated version of the article to the *Chicago Tribune*. While the estimated monetary value of enslaved laborers in the Dismal had dropped significantly to two thousand dollars, Raymond's sentiment remained consistent: "There is not one person residing in the south who is not familiar with 'the Virginia maroons.'"[2] To assume that every southerner had knowledge of the Dismal's maroons of course represented hyperbole. The preceding March, Frederick Street published a piece in *Frank Leslie's Popular Monthly* that included recent photographs of the Dismal Swamp. Hunters, Street explained, often stumbled on the ruins of the Dismal Swamp Land Company's old wooden plank shingle roads and "the remains of huts used years ago by runaway slaves." These camps, Street wrote, provided runaways not only with refuge but with access to "a safer, surer way of getting food." According to Street, runaways often cut timber, "work[ing] regularly in the gangs" with enslaved shinglers and "earn[ing] in return food, and powder and bullets, and occasionally enough, it is said, to buy their own freedom."[3] Tales of the Dismal's maroons persisted into the mid-twentieth century: novelist Bland Simpson, who grew up in North Carolina in the 1950s, remembered hearing about the maroons who inhabited the "implacable jungle" beyond the Dismal Canal: according to local lore, the swamp had once been "full of runaway slaves and escaped convicts that the law wouldn't follow in."[4]

Yet the Great Dismal was one of many swamps in the eastern tidewater regions of Virginia and North Carolina that came to feature prominently in the narrative of a former slave. Around the turn of the twentieth century, ex-slave William H. Robinson published a memoir, *From Log Cabin to the Pulpit; or, Fifteen Years in Slavery*. Robinson's title suggests the importance that he assigned to self-help and racial uplift, two themes that characterized the ways in which African American leaders sought to inspire the masses during the Jim Crow era.[5] In 1859, eleven-year-old William Cowens rescued his mother from a vicious beating by slaveholder Scott Cowens. The boy was heeding instructions from his father, Peter, who, prior to being separated from his family and sold to a slave trader had once lain "in the woods eleven months" in an effort to prevent William's mother from being whipped. Drawing inspiration from his father as well as from stories of other enslaved men's and women's "adventures" and "hiding places or rendezvous" in the woods, William fled into a swamp near Wilmington, North Carolina. There, he encountered scouts from a group of nineteen maroons who moved frequently within the swamp, and he ultimately spent three weeks with them.[6]

In his narrative, Robinson recalled "a low swampy place back of a thick cane brake." The remote location "was so dark and the cane so thick" that Robinson feared entering the place he had been instructed to find. Many dangers lurked in this pristine landscape:

> As I stood there I imagined I could hear the baying of blood hounds, and so strong was the imagination that it drove me in. I had several things to fear, for that country was infested with bears. More than once I had seen a bear come out of a corn field with his arms full of corn, go up to the fence and throw it over, pick it up like a man, and walk off. Then we had reptiles, such as water moccasins and rattle snakes. Sometimes I could walk upright, sometimes I was compelled to crawl through the cane. About three

o'clock the next morning I came out of the cane brake on the banks of a large pond of almost stagnant water. I could see the rocky mound or cave that I had heard so much talk of.[7]

William was placed under the direction of Uncle Amos, the camp's watch-man and prophet, who provided the boy with guidance and training in camp life. Several weeks later, Uncle Amos prophesized that the group would be discovered by slave catchers within three days and advised all members to move at once. Uncle Amos instructed each maroon to prepare arms and sup-plies to sustain them until they "learned something about the country sur-rounding" their new hiding place. Before the group could move, however, armed slave hunters discovered the camp after having worked "noiselessly all night" cutting their way through the cane to the maroon camp.[8]

After his capture, William was first sold at auction and subsequently re-sold to Joseph Cowens, Scott Cowens's brother and a Wilmington mer-chant. In April 1861, Joseph Cowens enlisted in the Confederate army, tak-ing William with him to Greenville, Tennessee, where Cowens was killed in late 1861 or early 1862. The boy remained an enslaved cook with the Confed-erate army until November 1863, when Union soldiers liberated him and he joined the U.S. forces. Less than a week later William and his mother were reunited in Greenville, and after accompanying the Union soldiers to Knox-ville, William purchased a small log cabin for his mother.[9]

Robinson served in the 54th Massachusetts and 28th Indiana Regiments until he mustered out in December 1865 and began his postwar life in Ten-nessee. After seventeen months driving a cart for a fire department, he "re-signed to accept a situation" as a singer and banjo player with the Tennes-see Singers, touring Tennessee, Indiana, Illinois, Michigan, Kentucky, and Windsor, Canada, with the group until it disbanded in November 1868. In January 1869, Hanlon's Wizard Oil Company hired William and seven oth-ers to a yearlong contract to give street concerts advertising the company. His travels with this troupe took him to New York City, and on May 21, 1869, he and his bandmates embarked for London. William S. Beckenworth then hired Robinson to detail the horrors of American slavery for various audi-ences. During his year in London, Robinson learned to read and write.[10]

Onboard a ship returning to the States, Robinson, now approximately age twenty-one, received additional tutoring from some fellow passengers, fueling his growing desire to learn. After landing in New York, Robinson made his way back to Nashville and enrolled in Central Tennessee College, a school established by the Methodist Episcopal Church under the auspices of the Freedmen's Bureau. William remained enrolled for three years, until his funds had been exhausted. Robinson found a teaching position in Lebanon, Tennessee, but it did not pay enough, so he went to work for the Woodruff Sleeping Car Company as a porter, spending the next few years traveling "every road of any importance in the United States and old and New Mexico."[11]

By the late 1870s, Robinson characterized himself as living the "miserable life" of a gambler in Chicago, pursuing not "self denial and perseverance" but "darkness, . . . immorality and sin." On January 1, 1877, Robinson, motivated by the disapproval his mother was sure to express once they were reunited, vowed to "get the religion of Jesus" into his heart. Robinson left Chicago and went to live with a Baptist preacher near La Porte, Indiana. Later in the same year, Robinson wed Alice Goins, of Riverside, Michigan, and they had three children before her death in April 1892.[12]

A member of the Missionary Baptist Church by the mid-1880s, Robinson explored his desire for conversion through the Baptist faith until 1891, when he joined Indianapolis's Simpson's Chapel Methodist Episcopal Church. Just prior to his wife's death, he was appointed an elder of the Methodist Episcopal Church in Shelbyville, Kentucky. For the next five years, William Robinson preached in Michigan, Indiana, and Illinois. During this period, Robinson was reunited with his mother and eight siblings, each of whom bore a different surname. They decided to "establish a family name and record" and took "Robinson" from the tale of Robinson Crusoe.[13]

When Robinson published his memoir at the turn of the twentieth century, he did so not to "bias the minds of the people or instill a spirit of hatred" but to reveal "the pathetic moan of slaves in almost utter despair, yet panting, groaning, bitterly wailing and still hoping for freedom." He intended his narrative to give voice to "slaves with their hearts lifted to God, praying for deliverance from the cruel bonds, the auction block, and years of unrequited grinding toil for those who had no right to their labor."[14]

Historians of nineteenth-century America have viewed the Civil War era as a significant break in the progression of American social, cultural, and political institutions, after which the nation reunified to reconcile the physical and institutional wounds the war had caused. On the one hand, historians have narrated the events that describe the ways that a postbellum generation of politicians, scholars, and public figures facilitated a political and economic Reconstruction to heal the nation's wounds. Reconciliation histories subordinated the deep-seated cultural, racial, and economic problems that had caused the Civil War in favor of progressive narratives that cast the nation's rebirth as a moment in which the South was born anew, in which the North had quickly outlawed slavery and emancipated enslaved people in the wake of the American Revolution, and in which the problem of slavery became a history of competition for the future of wage labor or enslavement.[15]

African Americans made significant gains during Reconstruction, though these gains were ultimately rescinded by violence and by the withdrawal of U.S. troops from the South after 1877. To bring attention to this postbellum truth, black Americans, former abolitionists, and their political allies articulated an emancipationist narrative in which the liberation of enslaved people was a central aim of a much broader project for full citizenship and equality. In this emancipationist vision, historians have focused on the lessons of the Reconstruction era in regard to African American history, generally explaining that the nation could not have reconciled its differences rooted in the injuries of slavery with new injustices against the gains of black civic and political rights during Reconstruction. In the wake of the disputed 1876 presidential election, Republicans and Democrats reached a compromise under which Rutherford B. Hayes received a term in the White House in exchange for the withdrawal of U.S. troops from the former states of the Confederacy. As southern Democrats "redeemed" state legislatures, the metaphorical gate to segregation was thrown open. Rising terrorism by the Ku Klux Klan, most evident in public lynchings of African Americans who sought civic and political enfranchisement, set the stage for the development of Jim Crow, which became firmly entrenched in 1896, when the U.S. Supreme Court's *Plessy v. Ferguson* decision upheld the doctrine of "separate but equal" in public accommodations. The black freedom struggle that seemed to have been fought and won in the 1860s and 1870s continued, eventually becoming the modern mid-twentieth-century civil rights movement.[16]

In the first three-quarters of the twentieth century, reconciliation held sway as the dominant narrative of the Civil War and Reconstruction. Robinson's account and numerous other narratives by former slaves were published at the height of the Jim Crow era, when proponents of the southern myth of the Lost Cause sought to advance a redemptive and revisionist version of the region's history.[17] By his own admission, Robinson sought for his narrative to strike a reconciliationist tone that also captured the long legacy of slavery's cruelties.

Yet Robinson's story also reflects the long legacy of marronage, a reminder that black resistance has deep roots in an Atlantic world history not bound by national sovereign claims. This is a key point that should be considered as historians continue to recast the boundaries of slavery not to reflect regional distinctions between North and South in the United States but rather to more accurately reflect the economic, political, and social networks that explicitly and complicitly bound the nation together, to emergent independent nations in the nineteenth-century global South, and to European nations that emerged during the Atlantic world's Age of Revolutions. As the Dismal's legacy of enslaved laborers and maroons demonstrates, this is not a theoretical exercise in the study of northern free black communities with an aim toward recasting them as maroon "communities of fugitives from slavery lodged in a society in which slavery still lived." Nor is it solely the study of a black resistance phenomenon distinctively African in character in a U.S. national context that serves as a counterpoint to "scholarly perspectives on slave cultures and forms of slave resistance" in North America, as historian Steven Hahn has suggested.[18] Rather, this effort is to engage even more fully the complexities of marronage in the southern United States in regional and in Atlantic world contexts.

That Robinson's story lends to a fuller understanding of American marronage illustrates the extent to which mobility—physical and otherwise—was central to his life. Robinson's narrative also disrupts the "inflexible historicist logic" that political scientist Neil Roberts has recently observed of histories of marronage and that this study has imposed on its reading of the Dismal Swamp Company's records.[19] In his early years, Robinson found refuge in a maroon camp in the swamps near Wilmington, not legally free but experiencing a modicum of freedom as he and Uncle Amos watched over the camp. Robinson subsequently became one of the thousands of enslaved black Americans who took up arms and fought to be free. His narrative of mobility in the postbellum era contributes to the long tradition of truth-telling documents intended to unveil the fables recast and retold by the progenitors of the South's Lost Cause.

Like the long black freedom struggle, the local legacies of petit marronage in North Carolina, Virginia, and the rest of the U.S. Southeast endured into the twentieth century and continue to inspire concepts of freedom into the twenty-first.

NOTES

ABBREVIATIONS

DSLC Records   Dismal Swamp Land Company Records, Financial, 1763–1789 and undated, David M. Rubenstein Rare Book and Manuscript Library, Duke University, Durham, North Carolina

LV   Library of Virginia, Richmond

Monroe Papers   Executive Papers of Governor James Monroe, 1799–1802, Accession 40936, Library of Virginia, Richmond

RBL   Richard Blow Letterbooks, Virginia Museum of History and Culture, Richmond

SANC   State Archives of North Carolina, Raleigh

INTRODUCTION

1. On the *Liberty Bell,* see Ralph Thompson, "The *Liberty Bell* and Other Antislavery Gift-Books," *New England Quarterly* 7, no. 1 (March 1934): 154–68.

2. Edmund Jackson, "The Virginia Maroons," *The Liberty Bell: By Friends of Freedom,* 1852, 143–51; Edmund Jackson, "Effects of Slavery," *The Liberty Bell: By Friends of Freedom,* 1842, 39–43; Edmund Jackson, "The Fugitive," *The Liberty Bell: By Friends of Freedom,* 1847, 5–15; Edmund Jackson, "Servile Insurrections," *The Liberty Bell: By Friends of Freedom,* 1851, 158–64. On Edmund Jackson, see Andrew Kull, *The Color-Blind Constitution* (Cambridge: Harvard University Press, 1998).

3. Edmund Jackson, "Virginia Maroons," 143–44; David Wheat, *Atlantic Africa and the Spanish Caribbean, 1570–1640* (Chapel Hill: University of North Carolina Press, 2016); José L. Franco, "Maroons and Slave Rebellions in the Spanish Territories," in *Maroon Societies: Rebel Slave Communities in the Americas,* ed. Richard Price (Baltimore: Johns Hopkins University Press, 1996), 35–48; Francisco Pérez de la Riva, "Cuban Palenques," in *Maroon Societies,* ed. Price, 49–59; Demoticus Philalethes, "Hunting the Maroons with Dogs in Cuba," in *Maroon Societies,* ed. Price, 60–63; M. L. E. Moreau de Saint-Méry, "The Border Maroons of Saint-Domingue: Le Maniel," in *Maroon Societies,* ed. Price, 135–42.

4. Dale W. Tomich, *Slavery in the Circuit of Sugar: Martinique and the World Econ-*

omy, 1830–1848 (Albany: State University of New York Press, 2016); Richard S. Dunn, *A Tale of Two Plantations: Slave Life and Labor in Jamaica and Virginia* (Cambridge: Harvard University Press, 2014); Richard S. Dunn, *Sugar and Slaves: The Rise of the Planter Class in the English West Indies, 1624–1713* (Chapel Hill: University of North Carolina Press, 2000); Simon P. Newman, *A New World of Labor: The Development of Plantation Slavery in the British Atlantic* (Philadelphia: University of Pennsylvania Press, 2013); Vincent Brown, *The Reaper's Garden: Death and Power in the World of Atlantic Slavery* (Cambridge: Harvard University Press, 2008); Russell Menard, *Sweet Negotiations: Sugar, Slavery, and Plantation Agriculture in Early Barbados* (Charlottesville: University of Virginia Press, 2006); Diana Paton, *No Bond but the Law: Punishment, Race, and Gender in Jamaican State Formation, 1780–1870* (Durham, N.C.: Duke University Press, 2004); Robert L. Paquette, *Sugar Is Made with Blood: The Conspiracy of La Escalera and the Conflict between Empires over Slavery in Cuba* (Middletown, Conn.: Wesleyan University Press, 1988); Sidney W. Mintz, *Sweetness and Power: The Place of Sugar in Modern History* (New York: Penguin, 1986); Stuart B. Schwartz, *Sugar Plantations in the Formation of Brazilian Society: Bahia, 1550–1835* (Cambridge: Cambridge University Press, 1985).

5. Michael Sivapragasam, "After the Treaties: A Social, Economic, and Demographic History of Maroon Society in Jamaica, 1739–1842" (PhD diss., University of Southampton, 2018); Tyson Reeder, "Liberty with the Sword: Jamaican Maroons, Haitian Revolutionaries, and American Liberty," *Journal of the Early Republic* 37, no. 1 (Spring 2017): 81–115; Daive A. Dunkley, *Agency of the Enslaved: Jamaica and the Culture of Freedom in the Atlantic World* (Lanham, Md.: Lexington Books, 2013); Alvin O. Thompson, *Flight to Freedom: African Runaways and Maroons in the Americas* (Kingston: University of the West Indies Press, 2006); Kenneth M. Bilby, *True-Born Maroons* (Gainesville: University Press of Florida, 2005); Karla Gotlieb, *A History of Queen Nanny: Leader of the Windward Maroons* (Trenton, N.J.: Africa World, 2000); Bev Carey, *The Maroon Story: The Authentic and Original History of the Maroons in the History of Jamaica, 1490–1880* (St. Andrew, Jamaica: Agouti, 1997); Mavis C. Campbell, *The Maroons of Jamaica, 1655–1796: A History of Resistance, Collaboration, and Betrayal* (Granby, Mass.: Bergin and Garvey, 1988).

6. Julius S. Scott, *The Common Wind: Afro-American Currents in the Age of the Haitian Revolution* (New York: Verso, 2018); Julius S. Scott, "The Common Wind: Currents of Afro-American Communication in the Era of the Haitian Revolution" (PhD diss., Duke University, 1986).

7. Harriet Beecher Stowe, *Dred: A Tale of the Great Dismal Swamp*, ed. Robert S. Levine (New York: Penguin, 2000); Joan D. Hedrick, *Harriet Beecher Stowe: A Life* (New York: Oxford University Press, 1994), 258–64.

8. Porte Crayon [David Hunter Strother], "Osman the Maroon in the Swamp," *Harper's New Monthly Magazine*, September 1856. For Strother, see Cecil D. Eby Jr., *"Porte Crayon": The Life of David Hunter Strother* (Chapel Hill: University of North Carolina Press, 1960).

9. Lawrence S. Earley, *Looking for Longleaf: The Fall and Rise of an American Forest* (Chapel Hill: University of North Carolina Press, 2004); Robert B. Outland III, *Tap-*

ping the Pines: The Naval Stores Industry in the American South (Baton Rouge: Louisiana State University Press, 2004); Robert B. Outland III, "Slavery, Work, and the Geography of the North Carolina Naval Stores Industry, 1835–1860," *Journal of Southern History* 62, no. 1 (February 1996): 27–56; Timothy Silver, *A New Face on the Countryside: Indians, Colonists, and Slaves in South Atlantic Forests, 1500–1800* (New York: Cambridge University Press, 1990); Peter C. Stewart, "The Shingle and Lumber Industries in the Great Dismal," *Journal of Forest History* 25, no. 2 (April 1981): 98–107; G. Melvin Herndon, "Forest Products of Colonial Georgia," *Journal of Forest History* 23, no. 3 (July 1979): 130–35; Donnie D. Bellamy, "Slavery in Microcosm: Onslow County, North Carolina," *Journal of Negro History* 62, no. 4 (October 1977): 339–50; Percival Perry, "The Naval-Stores Industry in the Old South, 1790–1860," *Journal of Southern History* 34, no. 4 (November 1968): 509–26; Sinclair Snow, "Naval Stores in Colonial Virginia," *Virginia Magazine of History and Biography* 72, no. 1 (January 1964): 75–93.

10. Daniel O. Sayers, *A Desolate Place for a Defiant People: The Archaeology of Maroons, Indigenous Americans, and Enslaved Laborers in the Great Dismal Swamp* (Gainesville: University Press of Florida, 2014), 114–99; Daniel O. Sayers, "Marronage Perspective for Historical Archaeology in the United States," *Historical Archaeology* 46, no. 4 (2012): 135–61; Daniel O. Sayers, "The Political Economy of Exile in the Great Dismal Swamp," *International Journal of Historical Archaeology* 11, no. 1 (2007): 60–97; Daniel O. Sayers, "The Diasporic World of the Great Dismal Swamp, 1630–1860" (PhD diss., College of William and Mary, 2008).

11. Becca Peixotto, "Wetlands in Defiance: Exploring African-American Resistance in the Great Dismal Swamp," *Journal of Wetland Archaeology* 17, no. 1 (September 2017): 18–35; Cynthia V. Goode, "Engaging the Tools of Resistance: Enslaved Africans' Tactics of Collective and Individual Consumption in Food, Medicine, and Clothing in the Great Dismal Swamp" (PhD diss., American University, 2016), 128.

12. David La Vere, *The Tuscarora War: Indians, Settlers, and the Fight for the Carolina Colonies* (Chapel Hill: University of North Carolina Press, 2013); Robin Beck, *Chiefdoms, Collapse, and Coalescence in the Early American South* (New York: Cambridge University Press, 2013); Edward DuBois Ragan, "'Scatter'd upon the English Seats': Indian Identity and Land Occupancy in the Rappahannock River Valley," in *Early Modern Virginia: Reconsidering the Old Dominion*, ed. Douglas Bradburn and John C. Coombs (Charlottesville: University of Virginia Press, 2011), 207–38; Noeleen McIlvenna, *A Very Mutinous People: The Struggle for North Carolina, 1660–1713* (Chapel Hill: University of North Carolina Press, 2009); Keith Egloff and Deborah Woodward, *First People: The Early Indians of Virginia*, 2nd ed. (Charlottesville: University of Virginia Press, 2006); Helen C. Roundtree, *Pocahantas, Powhatan, Opechancanough: Three Indian Lives Changed by Jamestown* (Charlottesville: University of Virginia Press, 2005); Helen C. Roundtree, *Powhatan Foreign Relations, 1500–1722* (Charlottesville: University Press of Virginia, 1993); Helen C. Roundtree, *The Powhatan Indians of Virginia: Their Traditional Culture* (Norman: University of Oklahoma Press, 1989); April Lee Hatfield, *Atlantic Virginia: Intercolonial Relations in the Seventeenth Century* (Philadelphia: University of Pennsylvania Press, 2004); Warren Billings, *Sir William Berkeley and the Forging of Colonial Virginia* (Baton Rouge:

Louisiana State University Press, 2004); Kirsten Fischer, *Suspect Relations: Sex, Race, and Resistance in Colonial North Carolina* (Ithaca: Cornell University Press, 2002); John K. Nelson, *A Blessed Company: Parishes, Parsons, and Parishioners in Anglican Virginia, 1690–1776* (Chapel Hill: University of North Carolina Press, 2001); Michael Leroy Oberg, *Dominion and Civility: English Imperialism and Native America, 1585–1685* (Ithaca: Cornell University Press, 1999); Frederic W. Gleach, *Powhatan's World and Colonial Virginia: A Conflict of Cultures* (Lincoln: University of Nebraska Press, 1997); Thomas C. Parramore, Peter C. Stewart, and Tommy L. Bogger, *Norfolk: The First Four Centuries* (Charlottesville: University Press of Virginia, 1994); J. Douglas Deal, *Race and Class in Colonial Virginia: Indians, Englishmen, and Africans on the Eastern Shore during the Seventeenth Century* (New York: Garland, 1993).

13. William Gooch to the Board of Trade, September 14, 1730, Colonial Office, Public Record Office, London 5/1322, 156, Virginia Colonial Records Project, LV; John Brickell, *The Natural History of North-Carolina* (Dublin: the Author, 1737), 356–57; Anthony S. Parent Jr. *Foul Means: The Formation of a Slave Society in Virginia, 1660–1740* (Chapel Hill: University of North Carolina Press, 2003): 160–61.

14. John J. Zaborney, *Slaves for Hire: Renting Enslaved Laborers in Antebellum Virginia* (Baton Rouge: Louisiana State University Press, 2012); Max Grivno, *Gleanings of Freedom: Free and Slave Labor along the Mason-Dixon Line, 1790–1860* (Urbana: University of Illinois Press, 2011); Seth Rockman, *Scraping By: Wage Labor, Slavery, and Survival in Early Baltimore* (Baltimore: Johns Hopkins University Press, 2009); Jonathan D. Martin, *Divided Mastery: Slave Hiring in the American South* (Cambridge: Harvard University Press, 2004); Darlene M. Perry, "A Profitable but Risky Business: Slave Hiring in Colonial and Antebellum Eastern North Carolina" (master's thesis, East Carolina University, 2004); Richard C. Wade, *Slavery in the Cities: The South, 1820–1860* (New York: Oxford University Press, 1964); Clement Eaton, *The Growth of Southern Civilization, 1790–1860* (New York: Harper and Row, 1963).

15. Steven Deyle, *Carry Me Back: The Domestic Slave Trade in American Life* (New York: Oxford University Press, 2005); Adam Rothman, *Slave Country: American Expansion and the Origins of the Deep South* (Cambridge: Harvard University Press, 2005); Robert H. Gudmestad, *A Troublesome Commerce: The Transformation of the Interstate Slave Trade* (Baton Rouge: Louisiana State University Press, 2003); Walter Johnson, *Soul by Soul: Life inside the Antebellum Slave Market* (Cambridge: Harvard University Press, 1999); Michael Tadman, *Speculators and Slaves: Masters, Traders, and Slaves in the Old South* (Madison: University of Wisconsin Press, 1996).

16. Marie Tyler-McGraw, *An African Republic: Black and White Virginians in the Making of Liberia* (Chapel Hill: University of North Carolina Press, 2007); Eric Burin, *Slavery and the Peculiar Solution* (Gainesville: University Press of Florida, 2005); Claude A. Klegg, *The Price of Liberty: African Americans and the Making of Liberia* (Chapel Hill: University of North Carolina Press, 2004).

17. Ted Maris-Wolf, "Hidden in Plain Sight: Maroon Life and Labor in Virginia's Dismal Swamp," *Slavery and Abolition* 34, no. 3 (2013): 446.

18. Loren Schweninger, "The Underside of Slavery: The Internal Economy, Self-

Hire, and Quasi-Freedom in Virginia, 1780–1865," *Slavery and Abolition* 12, no. 2 (1991): 1–22; John T. Schlotterbeck, "The Internal Economy of Slavery in Rural Piedmont Virginia," *Slavery and Abolition* 12, no. 1 (1991): 170–81.

19. Glenn Alan Cheney, *Quilombo dos Palmares: Brazil's Lost Nation of Fugitive Slaves* (Hanover, Conn.: New London Librarium, 2014); Yuko Miki, "Fleeing into Slavery: The Insurgent Geographies of Brazilian Quilombolas (Maroons), 1880–1881," *The Americas* 68, no. 4 (April 2012): 495–528; Timothy James Lockley, ed., *Maroon Communities in South Carolina: A Documentary Record* (Columbia: University of South Carolina Press, 2009); J. Brent Morris, "'Running Servants and All Others': The Diverse and Elusive Maroons of the Great Dismal Swamp," in *Voices from Within the Veil: African Americans and the Experience of Democracy*, ed. William Alexander, Cassandra Newby-Alexander, and Charles Ford (Newcastle-upon-Tyne: Cambridge Scholars, 2008), 85–112; Megan Kate Nelson, "Hidden Away in the Woods and Swamps: Slavery, Fugitive Slaves, and Swamplands in the Southeastern Borderlands, 1739–1845," in *"We Shall Independent Be": African American Place Making and the Struggle to Claim Space in the United States*, ed. Angel David Nieves and Leslie M. Alexander (Boulder: University Press of Colorado, 2008), 251–72; Erin Mackie, "Welcome to the Outlaw: Pirates, Maroons, and Caribbean Countercultures," *Cultural Critique* 59 (Winter 2005): 24–62; Jane Landers, *Black Society in Spanish Florida* (Urbana: University of Illinois Press, 1999); Thomas N. Ingersoll, *Mammon and Manon in Early New Orleans: The First Slave Society in the Deep South, 1718–1819* (Knoxville: University of Tennessee Press, 1999); Emilia Viotti da Costa, *Crowns of Glory, Tears of Blood: The Demerara Slave Rebellion of 1823* (New York: Oxford University Press, 1994); Kevin Mulroy, *Freedom on the Border: The Seminole Maroons in Florida, the Indian Territory, Coahuila, and Texas* (Lubbock: Texas Tech University Press, 1993); Gwendolyn Midlo Hall, *Africans in Colonial Louisiana: The Development of Afro-Creole Culture in the Eighteenth Century* (Baton Rouge: Louisiana State University Press, 1992); Patrick J. Carroll, "Mandinga: The Evolution of a Mexican Runaway Slave Community, 1735–1827," *Comparative Studies in Society and History* 19, no. 4 (October 1977): 488–505.

20. Price, *Maroon Societies*, 1–5.

21. Eric Williams, *Capitalism and Slavery* (Chapel Hill: University of North Carolina Press, 1994).

22. David W. Galenson, *Traders, Planters, and Slaves: Market Behavior in Early English America* (Cambridge: Cambridge University Press, 1986); Daniel C. Littlefield, *Rice and Slaves: Ethnicity and the Slave Trade in Colonial South Carolina* (Urbana: University of Illinois Press, 1981); Philip D. Curtin, *The Atlantic Slave Trade: A Census* (Madison: University of Wisconsin Press, 1969).

23. John Hope Franklin, *The Militant South* (Boston: Beacon, 1956); John Hope Franklin, *The Free Negro in North Carolina, 1790–1860* (Chapel Hill: University of North Carolina Press, 1943); Herbert Aptheker, *American Negro Slave Revolts: On Nat Turner, Denmark Vesey, Gabriel, and Others*, 50th anniv. ed. (New York: International, 1993); Herbert Aptheker, "Maroons within the Present Limits of the United States," *Journal of Negro History* 24, no. 2 (April 1939): 167–84.

24. Stanley M. Elkins, *Slavery: A Problem in American Institutional and Intellectual Life*, 2nd ed. (Chicago: University of Chicago Press, 1968); Kenneth M. Stampp, *The Peculiar Institution: Slavery in the Ante-bellum South* (New York: Vintage, 1956).

25. David Brion Davis, *Inhuman Bondage: The Rise and Fall of Slavery in the New World* (New York: Oxford University Press, 2006); David Brion Davis, *Slavery and Human Progress* (New York: Oxford University Press, 1984); David Brion Davis, *The Problem of Slavery in the Age of Revolution, 1770–1823* (Ithaca: Cornell University Press, 1975); David Brion Davis, *The Problem of Slavery in Western Culture* (Ithaca: Cornell University Press, 1967); Philip D. Morgan, *Slave Counterpoint: Black Culture in the Eighteenth-Century Chesapeake and Lowcountry* (Chapel Hill: University of North Carolina Press, 1998); Ira Berlin and Philip D. Morgan, "Introduction: Labor and the Shaping of Slave Life in the Americas," in *Cultivation and Culture: Labor and the Shaping of Slave Life in the Americas*, ed. Ira Berlin and Philip D. Morgan (Charlottesville: University Press of Virginia, 1993), 1–45; Philip D. Morgan, "Slave Life in Piedmont Virginia, 1720–1800," in *Colonial Chesapeake Society*, ed. Lois Green Carr, Philip D. Morgan, and Jean B. Russo (Chapel Hill: University of North Carolina Press, 1988), 433–84; Philip D. Morgan, "Work and Culture: The Task System and the World of Lowcountry Blacks, 1700 to 1880," *William and Mary Quarterly*, 3rd ser., 39, no. 4 (1982): 564–99; Ira Berlin, *The Making of African America: The Four Great Migrations* (New York: Penguin, 2010); Ira Berlin, *Generations of Captivity: A History of African-American Slaves* (Cambridge: Belknap Press of Harvard University Press, 2003); Ira Berlin, "From Creole to African: Atlantic Creoles and the Origins of African American Society in Mainland North America," *William and Mary Quarterly*, 3rd ser., 53, no. 2 (April 1996): 251–288; Ira Berlin and Herbert G. Gutman, "Natives and Immigrants, Free Men and Slaves: Urban Workingmen in the Antebellum South," *American Historical Review* 88, no. 5 (December 1983): 1175–1200; Ira Berlin, "Time, Space, and the Evolution of Afro-American Society on British Mainland North America," *American Historical Review* 85, no. 1 (February 1980): 44–78; Ira Berlin, *Slaves without Masters: The Free Negro in the Antebellum South* (New York: New Press, 2007); Edmund S. Morgan, *American Slavery, American Freedom* (1974; rpt., New York: Norton, 1975); Edmund S. Morgan, "Slavery and Freedom: The American Paradox," *Journal of American History* 59, no. 1 (June 1972): 5–29.

26. John C. Coombs, "Beyond the 'Origins Debate': Rethinking the Rise of Virginia Slavery," in *Early Modern Virginia*, ed. Bradburn and Coombs, 239–78; William A. Pettigrew, "Transatlantic Politics and the Africanization of Virginia's Labor Force, 1688–1712," in *Early Modern Virginia*, ed. Bradburn and Coombs, 279–99; Jeff Forret, *Race Relations at the Margins: Slaves and Poor Whites in the Antebellum Southern Countryside* (Baton Rouge: Louisiana State University Press, 2006); Melvin Patrick Ely, *Israel on the Appomattox: A Southern Experiment in Black Freedom from the 1790s through the Civil War* (New York: Vintage, 2004); Peter Kolchin, *American Slavery, 1619–1877* (New York: Hill and Wang, 2003); Trevor Burnard, *Creole Gentlemen: The Maryland Elite, 1691–1776* (New York: Routledge, 2002); David S. Cecelski, *The Waterman's Song: Slavery and Freedom in Maritime North Carolina* (Chapel Hill: University of North Carolina Press, 2001); Timothy James Lockley, *Lines in the Sand:*

Race and Class in Lowcountry Georgia, 1750–1860 (Athens: University of Georgia Press, 2001); W. Jeffrey Bolster, *Black Jacks: African American Seamen in the Age of Sail* (Cambridge: Harvard University Press, 1997); Thomas D. Morris, *Southern Slavery and the Law, 1619–1860* (Chapel Hill: University of North Carolina Press, 1996); S. Charles Bolton, *Arkansas, 1800–1860* (Fayetteville: University of Arkansas Press, 1998); Whittington B. Johnson, *Black Savannah, 1788–1864* (Fayetteville: University of Arkansas Press, 1996); Stephanie McCurry, *Masters of Small Worlds: Yeoman Households, Gender Relations, and the Political Culture of the Antebellum South Carolina Low Country* (New York: Oxford University Press, 1995); James Horn, *Adapting to a New World: English Society in the Seventeenth-Century Chesapeake* (Chapel Hill: University of North Carolina Press, 1994); Lorena S. Walsh, "Slave Life, Slave Society, and Tobacco Production in the Tidewater Chesapeake, 1620–1820," in *Cultivation and Culture*, ed. Berlin and Morgan, 170–99; Lynda J. Morgan, *Emancipation in Virginia's Tobacco Belt, 1850–1870* (Athens: University of Georgia Press, 1992); Bill Cecil-Fronsman, *Common Whites: Class and Culture in Antebellum North Carolina* (Lexington: University Press of Kentucky, 1992); Allan Kulikoff, *Tobacco and Slaves: The Development of Southern Cultures in the Chesapeake, 1680–1800* (Chapel Hill: University of North Carolina Press, 1986); Barbara Jeanne Fields, *Slavery and Freedom on the Middle Ground: Maryland during the Nineteenth Century* (New Haven: Yale University Press, 1985); Darrett B. Rutman and Anita H. Rutman, *A Place in Time: Middlesex County, Virginia, 1650–1750* (New York: Norton, 1984); T. H. Breen and Stephen Innes, *"Myne Owne Ground": Race and Freedom on Virginia's Eastern Shore, 1640–1676* (New York: Oxford University Press, 1980).

27. Kathleen DuVal, *Independence Lost: Lives on the Edge of the American Revolution* (New York: Random House, 2016); Claudio Saunt, *West of the Revolution: An Uncommon History of 1776* (New York: Norton, 2014); Emily Blanck, *Tyrannicide: Forging an American Law of Slavery in Revolutionary South Carolina and Massachusetts* (Athens: University of Georgia Press, 2014); T. H. Breen, *American Insurgents, American Patriots: The Revolution of the People* (New York: Hill and Wang, 2010); Patrick Griffin, *American Leviathan: Empire, Nation, and American Frontier* (New York: Hill and Wang, 2007); Gary B. Nash, *The Unknown American Revolution: The Unruly Birth of Democracy and the Struggle to Create America* (New York: Penguin, 2005); Robert A. Gross, *The Minutemen and Their World*, 25th anniv. ed. (New York: Hill and Wang, 2001); Jon Butler, *Becoming America: The Revolution before 1776* (Cambridge: Harvard University Press, 2000); Peter H. Wood, "'Liberty Is Sweet': African-American Freedom Struggles in the Years before White Independence," in *Beyond the American Revolution: Explorations in the History of American Radicalism*, ed. Alfred F. Young (DeKalb: Northern Illinois University Press, 1993), 149–84; Sylvia R. Frey, *Water from the Rock: Black Resistance in a Revolutionary Age* (Princeton: Princeton University Press, 1991); Sylvia R. Frey, "Between Slavery and Freedom: Virginia Blacks in the American Revolution," *Journal of Southern History* 49, no. 3 (August 1983): 375–98; Marvin L. Michael Kay and Lorin Lee Cary, "Class, Mobility, and Conflict in North Carolina on the Eve of the Revolution," in *The Southern Experience in the American Revolution*, ed. Jeffrey J. Crow and Larry E. Tise (Chapel Hill: University of North Carolina Press,

1978), 109–54; Bernard Bailyn, *The Ideological Origins of the American Revolution*, en-
larged ed. (Cambridge: Harvard University Press, 1992); Norman K. Risjord, *Jefferson's
America, 1760–1815* (Madison, Wis.: Madison House, 1991); John Shy, "The American
Revolution: The Military Conflict Considered as a Revolutionary War," in *Essays on
the American Revolution*, ed. Stephen G. Kurtz and James H. Hutson (Chapel Hill:
University of North Carolina Press, 1973), 121–56; Benjamin Quarles, *The Negro in the
American Revolution* (Chapel Hill: University of North Carolina Press, 1961); Wil-
liam Cooper Nell, *The Colored Patriots of the American Revolution with Sketches of Several Distinguished Colored Persons* (Boston: Walcutt, 1855).

28. Alan Taylor, *The Internal Enemy: Slavery and War in Virginia, 1772–1832* (New
York: Norton, 2013); Michael A. McDonnell, *The Politics of War: Race, Class, and Con-
flict in Revolutionary Virginia* (Chapel Hill: University of North Carolina Press, 2007);
Rhys Isaac, *Landon Carter's Uneasy Kingdom: Revolution and Rebellion on a Virginia
Plantation* (New York: Oxford University Press, 2004); James Sidbury, *Ploughshares
into Swords: Race, Rebellion, and Identity in Gabriel's Virginia, 1730–1810* (New York:
Cambridge University Press, 1997); Woody Holton, *Forced Founders: Indians, Debtors,
Slaves, and the Making of the American Revolution in Virginia* (Chapel Hill: University
of North Carolina Press, 1999); James Titus, *The Old Dominion at War: Society, Politics,
and Warfare in Late Colonial Virginia* (Columbia: University of South Carolina Press,
1991).

29. Ryan A. Quintana, *Making a Slave State: Political Development in Early South
Carolina* (Chapel Hill: University of North Carolina Press, 2018); Christy Clark-
Pujara, *Dark Work: The Business of Slavery in Rhode Island* (New York: New York Uni-
versity Press, 2016); Rashauna Johnson, *Slavery's Metropolis: Unfree Labor in New Or-
leans during the Age of Revolutions* (New York: Cambridge University Press, 2016);
Jared Ross Hardesty, *Unfreedom: Slavery and Dependence in Eighteenth-Century Boston*
(New York: New York University Press, 2016); Wendy Warren, *New England Bound:
Slavery and Colonization in Early America* (New York: Liveright, 2016); Margaret El-
len Newell, *Brethren by Nature: New England Indians, Colonists, and the Origins of
American Slavery* (Ithaca: Cornell University Press, 2015).

30. Emily Clark, *The Strange History of the American Quadroon: Free Women of Color
in the Revolutionary Atlantic World* (Chapel Hill: University of North Carolina Press,
2013); Rebecca J. Scott and Jean M. Hébrard, *Freedom Papers: An Atlantic Odyssey
in the Age of Emancipation* (Cambridge: Harvard University Press, 2012); Thavolia
Glymph, *Out of the House of Bondage: The Transformation of the Plantation Household*
(New York: Cambridge University Press, 2008); Daina Ramey Berry, *Swing the Sickle
for the Harvest Is Ripe: Gender and Slavery in Antebellum Georgia* (Urbana: University
of Illinois Press, 2007); Stephanie M. H. Camp, *Closer to Freedom: Enslaved Women
and Everyday Resistance in the Plantation South* (Chapel Hill: University of North
Carolina Press, 2004); Jennifer L. Morgan, *Laboring Women: Reproduction and Gender
in New World Slavery* (Philadelphia: University of Pennsylvania Press, 2004); Joshua
D. Rothman, *Notorious in the Neighborhood: Sex and Families across the Color Line in
Virginia, 1787–1861* (Chapel Hill: University of North Carolina Press, 2003); Kathleen
M. Brown, *Good Wives, Nasty Wenches, and Anxious Patriarchs: Gender, Race, and Power*

in Colonial Virginia (Chapel Hill: University of North Carolina Press, 1996); Nell Irvin Painter, *Sojourner Truth: A Life, A Symbol* (New York: Norton, 1996); Brenda E. Stevenson, *Life in Black and White: Family and Community in the Slave South* (New York: Oxford University Press, 1996); Deborah Gray White, *Ar'n't I a Woman?: Female Slaves in the Plantation South* (New York: Norton, 1985); Suzanne Lebsock, *The Free Women of Petersburg: Status and Culture in a Southern Town, 1784–1860* (New York: Norton, 1984).

31. Andrew K. Diemer, *The Politics of Black Citizenship: Free African Americans in the Mid-Atlantic Borderland, 1817–1863* (Athens: University of Georgia Press, 2016); Cheryl Janifer LaRoche, *Free Black Communities and the Underground Railroad: The Geography of Resistance* (Urbana: University of Illinois Press, 2014); Amrita Chakrabarti Myers, *Forging Freedom: Black Women and the Pursuit of Liberty in Antebellum Charleston* (Chapel Hill: University of North Carolina Press, 2011); Elise Lemire, *Black Walden: Slavery and Its Aftermath in Concord, Massachusetts* (Philadelphia: University of Pennsylvania Press, 2009); Leslie M. Alexander, *African or American?: Black Identity and Political Activism in New York City, 1784–1861* (Urbana: University of Illinois Press, 2008); Sylviane A. Diouf, *Dreams of Africa in Alabama: The Slave Ship Clotilda and the Story of the Last Africans Brought to America* (New York: Oxford University Press, 2007); Leslie M. Harris, *In the Shadow of Slavery: African Americans in New York City, 1626–1863* (Chicago: University of Chicago Press, 2003); Craig Steven Wilder, *In the Company of Black Men: The African Influence on African American Culture in New York City* (New York: New York University Press, 2001); Graham Russell Hodges, *Root and Branch: African Americans in New York and East Jersey, 1613–1863* (Chapel Hill: University of North Carolina Press, 1999); Kimberly S. Hanger, *Bounded Lives, Bounded Places: Free Black Society in Colonial New Orleans, 1769–1803* (Durham, N.C.: Duke University Press, 1997); James Oliver Horton and Lois E. Horton, *In Hope of Liberty: Culture, Community, and Protest among Northern Free Blacks, 1700–1860* (New York: Oxford University Press, 1997); Christopher Phillips, *Freedom's Port: The African American Community of Baltimore, 1790–1860* (Urbana: University of Illinois Press, 1997); Tommy L. Bogger, *Free Blacks in Norfolk, Virginia, 1790–1860: The Darker Side of Freedom* (Charlottesville: University of Virginia Press, 1997); Gary B. Nash, *Forging Freedom: The Formation of Philadelphia's Black Community, 1720–1840* (Cambridge: Harvard University Press, 1988).

32. Vincent Harding, *There Is a River: The Black Struggle for Freedom in America* (San Diego: Harcourt Brace, 1981), xix; Margaret Creel Washington, *A Peculiar People: Slave Religion and Community-Culture among the Gullahs* (New York: New York University Press, 1988); Sterling Stuckey, *Slave Culture: Nationalist Theory and the Foundations of Black America* (New York: Oxford University Press, 1987); Sterling Stuckey, "Through the Prism of Folklore: The Black Ethos in Slavery," *Massachusetts Review* 9, no. 3 (Summer 1968): 417–37; Herbert Aptheker, "Resistance and Afro-American History: Some Notes on Contemporary Historiography and Suggestions for Further Research," in *In Resistance: Studies in African, Caribbean, and Afro-American History*, ed. Gary Y. Okihiro (Amherst: University of Massachusetts Press, 1986), 10–20; Charles Joyner, *Down by the Riverside: A South Carolina Slave Community* (Urbana:

University of Illinois Press, 1984); John Scott Strickland, "The Great Revival and In-surrectionary Fears in North Carolina: An Examination of Antebellum Southern Society and Slave Revolt Panics," in *Class, Conflict, and Consensus: Antebellum South-ern Community Studies*, ed. Orville Vernon Burton and Robert C. McMath Jr. (West-port, Conn.: Greenwood, 1982), 57–95; Leonard P. Curry, *The Free Black in Urban America, 1800–1850: The Shadow of the Dream* (Chicago: University of Chicago Press, 1981); Mechal Sobel, *Trabelin' On: The Slave Journey to an Afro-Baptist Faith* (Prince-ton: Princeton University Press, 1979); Eugene D. Genovese, *From Rebellion to Revo-lution: Afro-American Slave Revolts in the Making of the New World* (New York: Vin-tage, 1979); Eugene Genovese, *Roll, Jordan, Roll: The World the Slaves Made* (New York: Vintage, 1976); Eugene Genovese, *The Political Economy of Slavery: Studies in the Econ-omy and Society of the Slave South* (New York: Vintage, 1965); Thomas L. Webber, *Deep Like the Rivers: Education in the Slave Quarter Community, 1831–1865* (New York: Norton, 1978); Herbert G. Gutman, *The Black Family in Slavery and Freedom, 1750–1925* (New York: Pantheon, 1976); Peter H. Wood, *Black Majority: Negroes in Colonial South Carolina from 1670 through the Stono Rebellion* (New York: Norton, 1974); John W. Blassingame, *The Slave Community: Plantation Life in the Antebellum South* (New York: Oxford University Press, 1972); George P. Rawick, *From Sundown to Sunup: The Making of the Black Community* (Westport, Conn.: Greenwood, 1972); Leon F. Lit-wack, *North of Slavery: The Negro in the Free States, 1790–1860* (Chicago: University of Chicago Press, 1961).

33. Gerald Horne, *The Counter-Revolution of 1776: Slave Resistance and the Origins of the United States of America* (New York: New York University Press, 2014); Jason R. Young, *Rituals of Resistance: African Atlantic Religion in the Kongo and in the Lowcoun-try South in the Era of Slavery* (Baton Rouge: Louisiana State University Press, 2007); Walter C. Rucker, *The River Flows On: Black Resistance, Culture, and Identity Forma-tion in Early America* (Baton Rouge: Louisiana State University Press, 2006); Chris-topher Leslie Brown and Philip D. Morgan, eds., *Arming Slaves: From Classical Times to the Modern Age* (New Haven: Yale University Press, 2006); Michael A. Gomez, *Re-versing Sail: A History of the African Diaspora* (New York: Cambridge University Press, 2005); Michael A. Gomez, *Exchanging Our Country Marks: The Transformation of Af-rican Identities in the Colonial and Antebellum South* (Chapel Hill: University of North Carolina Press, 1998); Michael Mullin, *Africa in America: Slave Acculturation and Re-sistance in the American South and the British Caribbean, 1736–1831* (Urbana: University of Illinois Press, 1992).

34. Sharla M. Fett, *Recaptured Africans: Surviving Slave Ships, Detention, and Dis-location in the Final Years of the Slave Trade* (Chapel Hill: University of North Caro-lina Press, 2017); Randy M. Browne, *Surviving Slavery in the British Caribbean* (Phil-adelphia: University of Pennsylvania Press, 2017); Sowandé M. Mustakeem, *Slavery at Sea: Terror, Sex, and Sickness in the Middle Passage* (Urbana: University of Illinois Press, 2016); Gregory E. O'Malley, *Final Passages: The Intercolonial Slave Trade of Brit-ish America, 1619–1807* (Chapel Hill: University of North Carolina Press, 2014); Greg-ory E. O'Malley, "Slavery's Converging Ground: Charleston's Slave Trade as the Black Heart of the Low Country," *William and Mary Quarterly*, 3rd ser., 74, no. 2

(April 2017): 271–302; Patrick Manning, *The African Diaspora: A History through Culture* (New York: Columbia University Press, 2009); Alexander X. Byrd, *Captives and Voyagers: Black Migrants across the Eighteenth-Century British Atlantic World* (Baton Rouge: Louisiana State University Press, 2008); Marcus Rediker, *The Slave Ship: A Human History* (New York: Penguin, 2008); Stephanie E. Smallwood, *Saltwater Slavery: A Middle Passage from Africa to American Diaspora* (Cambridge: Harvard University Press, 2007); Daniel C. Littlefield, *Rice and Slaves: Ethnicity and the Slave Trade in Colonial South Carolina* (Urbana: University of Illinois Press, 1981); Philip D. Curtin, *The Atlantic Slave Trade: A Census* (Madison: University of Wisconsin Press, 1969).

35. Ronald L. Heinemann, John G. Kolp, Anthony S. Parent Jr., and William G. Shade, *Old Dominion, New Commonwealth: A History of Virginia, 1607–2007* (Charlottesville: University of Virginia Press, 2007), 136–37; Marvin L. Michael Kay and Lorin Lee Cary, *Slavery in North Carolina, 1748–1775* (Chapel Hill: University of North Carolina Press, 1995).

36. Tyler-McGraw, *African Republic*; Eva Sheppard Wolf, *Race and Liberty in the New Nation: Emancipation in Virginia from the Revolution to Nat Turner's Rebellion* (Baton Rouge: Louisiana State University Press, 2006); Burin, *Slavery and the Peculiar Solution*; Klegg, *Price of Liberty*.

37. Edward B. Rugemer, *Slave Law and the Politics of Resistance in the Early Atlantic World* (Cambridge: Harvard University Press, 2018); Edward B. Rugemer, *The Problem of Emancipation: The Caribbean Roots of the American Civil War* (Baton Rouge: Louisiana State University Press, 2009); Patrick Rael, *Eighty-Eight Years: The Long Death of Slavery in the United States, 1777–1865* (Athens: University of Georgia Press, 2015); Patrick Rael, *Black Identity and Black Protest in the Antebellum North* (Chapel Hill: University of North Carolina Press, 2002); W. Caleb McDaniel, *The Problem of Democracy in the Age of Slavery: Garrisonian Abolitionists and Transatlantic Reform* (Baton Rouge: Louisiana State University Press, 2013); Robin Blackburn, *The American Crucible: Slavery, Emancipation, and Human Rights* (London: Verso, 2011); Seymour Drescher, *Abolition: A History of Slavery and Antislavery* (New York: Cambridge University Press, 2009); Maurice Jackson, *Let this Voice Be Heard: Anthony Benezet, Father of Atlantic Abolitionism* (Philadelphia: University of Pennsylvania Press, 2009); James Brewer Stewart, *Abolitionist Politics and the Coming of the Civil War* (Amherst: University of Massachusetts Press, 2008); Christopher Leslie Brown, *Moral Capital: Foundations of British Abolitionism* (Chapel Hill: University of North Carolina Press, 2006); Richard S. Newman, *The Transformation of American Abolitionism: Fighting Slavery in the Early Republic* (Chapel Hill: University of North Carolina Press, 2002); Julie Roy Jeffrey, *The Great Silent Army of Abolitionism: Ordinary Women in the Antislavery Movement* (Chapel Hill: University of North Carolina Press, 1998); Bertram Wyatt-Brown, *Lewis Tappan and the Evangelical War against Slavery* (Baton Rouge: Louisiana State University Press, 1997); Jean Fagan Yellin and John C. Van Horne, eds., *The Abolitionist Sisterhood: Women's Political Culture in Antebellum America* (Ithaca: Cornell University Press, 1994); Merton L. Dillon, *Slavery Attacked: Southern States and Their Allies, 1619–1865* (Baton Rouge: Louisiana State University Press, 1990); Merton L. Dillon, *The Abolitionists: The Growth of a Dissenting Minority*

(DeKalb: Northern Illinois University Press, 1974); David Brion Davis, "Reflections on Abolitionism and Ideological Hegemony," *American Historical Review* 92, no. 4 (October 1987): 797–812; R. J. M. Blackett, *Building an Antislavery Wall: Black Americans in the Atlantic Abolitionist Movement* (Baton Rouge: Louisiana State University Press, 1983); Ronald G. Walters, *The Antislavery Appeal: American Abolitionism after 1830* (New York: Norton, 1978); Ronald G. Walters, *American Reformers, 1815–1860* (New York: Hill and Wang, 1978); Winthrop D. Jordan, *The White Man's Burden: Historical Origins of Racism in the United States* (New York: Oxford University Press, 1974); Winthrop D. Jordan, *White over Black: American Attitudes toward the Negro, 1550–1812* (Chapel Hill: University of North Carolina Press, 1968); Arthur Zilversmit, *The First Emancipation: The Abolition of Slavery in the North* (Chicago: University of Chicago Press, 1967); Carl N. Degler, *Neither Black nor White: Slavery and Race Relations in Brazil and the United States* (Madison: University of Wisconsin Press, 1971); Carl N. Degler, "Slavery and the Genesis of American Race Prejudice," *Comparative Studies in Society and History* 2, no. 1 (October 1959): 49–66.

38. Sven Beckert and Christine Desan, eds., *American Capitalism: New Histories* (New York: Columbia University Press, 2018); Sven Beckert, *Empire of Cotton: A Global History* (New York: Vintage, 2014).

39. Daina Ramey Berry, *The Price for Their Pound of Flesh: The Value of the Enslaved, from Womb to Grave, in the Building of a Nation* (Boston: Beacon, 2017); Calvin Schermerhorn, *The Business of Slavery and the Rise of American Capitalism, 1815–1860* (New Haven: Yale University Press, 2015); Calvin Schermerhorn, *Money over Mastery, Family over Freedom: Slavery in the Antebellum Upper South* (Baltimore: Johns Hopkins University Press, 2011); Edward E. Baptist, *The Half Has Never Been Told: Slavery and the Making of American Capitalism* (New York: Basic Books, 2014); Joshua D. Rothman, *Flush Times and Fever Dreams: A Story of Capitalism and Slavery in the Age of Jackson* (Athens: University of Georgia Press, 2012).

40. Walter Johnson, *River of Dark Dreams: Slavery and Empire in the Cotton Kingdom* (Cambridge: Belknap Press of Harvard University Press, 2013), 9–10.

41. Sven Beckert and Seth Rockman, eds., *Slavery's Capitalism: A New History of American Economic Development* (Philadelphia: University of Pennsylvania Press, 2016), 1.

42. Thomas Wentworth Higginson, "Memoir of Thomas Wentworth Higginson," in *Army Life in a Black Regiment* (Boston: Osgood, 1870), 296; Nathaniel Millett, *The Maroons of Prospect Bluff and Their Quest for Freedom in the Atlantic World* (Gainesville: University Press of Florida, 2013), 1. According to Millett, the fort's peak population numbered in the hundreds and included men, women, and children from the African and Indian diasporas of the Gulf Coast. They lived in British-built, well-constructed houses; cultivated fields; participated in an exchange economy; organized a militia for defense; and developed a political system.

43. Sylviane A. Diouf, *Slavery's Exiles: The Story of the American Maroons* (New York: New York University Press, 2014). Diouf's framing of maroon "settlement" in the Dismal builds on Hugo P. Leaming's *Hidden Americans*, in which Leaming contended that a permanent maroon community remained entrenched in the Dismal

from the mid-seventeenth century until the Civil War. In Leaming's view, core maroon communities with clearly defined social customs incorporated new escapees from surrounding plantations. These settlements developed in concentric circles radiating outward from the swamp's center over time, with the most remote communities always remaining deeply entrenched. See Hugo P. Leaming, *Hidden Americans: Maroons of Virginia and the Carolinas* (New York: Garland, 1993).

Some historians have rejected Leaming's observations, with the most pointed critique citing a number of critical errors in analysis and interpretation of primary source material and historical context. Peter C. Stewart has observed that *Hidden Americans* contains errors in numerical sequence regarding the counting of years and population figures and an erroneous interpretation of the Revolutionary War battle at Kemp's Landing in Princess Anne County, which Leaming describes as a victory for "a band of African Americans and poor whites" over the local militia although the skirmish actually involved more than one hundred Redcoats and "dozens of Norfolk merchants and Princess Anne County planters." See Peter C. Stewart, review of *Hidden Americans: Maroons of Virginia and the Carolinas*, by Hugo P. Leaming, *William and Mary Quarterly* 53, no. 3 (July 1996): 666–67.

44. Frederick Douglass, "Slaves in the Dismal Swamp," *North Star*, March 31, 1848.

45. I borrow the term "freedom's seekers" from historian Jeffrey R. Kerr-Ritchie, *Freedom's Seekers: Essays on Comparative Emancipation* (Baton Rouge: Louisiana State University Press, 2013).

46. Manisha Sinha, *The Slave's Cause: A History of Abolition* (New Haven: Yale University Press, 2016); Benjamin Quarles, *Black Abolitionists* (New York: Oxford University Press, 1969).

47. Kathleen M. Hilliard, *Masters, Slaves, and Exchange: Power's Purchase in the Old South* (New York: Cambridge University Press, 2014); Roger D. Abrahams, *Singing the Master: The Emergence of African-American Culture in the Plantation South* (New York: Penguin, 1993); Drew Gilpin Faust, *James Henry Hammond and the Old South: A Design for Mastery* (Baton Rouge: Louisiana State University Press, 1982).

48. Marisa J. Fuentes, *Dispossessed Lives: Enslaved Women, Violence, and the Archive* (Philadelphia: University of Pennsylvania Press, 2016), 1–12.

Other historians and scholars have used similar methods to examine historical records of enslaved people in the attempt to produce richer, more robust histories of slavery and oppression. See Browne, *Surviving Slavery*; Ann Laura Stoler, *Along the Archival Grain: Epistemic Anxieties and Colonial Common Sense* (Princeton: Princeton University Press, 2009); Saidiya Hartman, *Scenes of Subjection: Terror, Slavery, and Self-Making in Nineteenth-Century America* (New York: Oxford University Press, 1997); Michel-Rolph Trouillot, *Silencing the Past: Power and the Production of History* (Boston: Beacon, 1995); James Scott, *Domination and the Arts of Resistance: Hidden Transcripts* (New Haven: Yale University Press, 1990).

49. Carole Watterson Troxler, "Land Tenure as a Regulator Grievance and Revolutionary Tool," in *New Voyages to Carolina: Reinterpreting North Carolina History*, ed. Larry E. Tise and Jeffrey J. Crow (Chapel Hill: University of North Carolina Press, 2017), 110–43; Marjoleine Kars, *Breaking Loose Together: The Regulator Rebel-*

lion in Pre-Revolutionary North Carolina (Chapel Hill: University of North Carolina Press, 2002).

PROLOGUE. "LURKING IN SWAMPS, WOODS, OR OTHER OBSCURE PLACES"

1. Anthony S. Parent Jr., *Foul Means: The Formation of a Slave Society in Virginia, 1660–1740* (Chapel Hill: University of North Carolina Press, 2003), 161–62; John Brickell, *The Natural History of North-Carolina* (Dublin: the Author, 1743), 357.

2. John Ferdinand Dalziel Smyth, *A Tour in the United States of America* (Dublin: Price, Moncrieffe, 1784), 2:101.

3. William Byrd II, *The History of the Dividing Line betwixt Virginia and N. Carolina Run in the Year of Our Lord 1728* (Alexandria, Va.: Alexander Street, 1728), 43–45. See also Jacqueline A. Martin, "The Maroons of the Great Dismal Swamp, 1607–1865" (master's thesis, Western Washington University, 2004).

4. Alan Gallay, *The Indian Slave Trade: The Rise of the English Empire in the American South, 1670–1717* (New Haven: Yale University Press, 2002).

5. Jacqueline A. Martin, "Maroons," 47–52; Arwin D. Smallwood, "A History of Native American and African Relations from 1502 to 1900," *Negro History Bulletin* 62, nos. 2–3 (April–September 1999): 18–31; Arwin D. Smallwood, "A History of Three Cultures: Indian Woods, North Carolina 1585 to 1995" (PhD diss., Ohio State University, 1998).

6. Sally E. Hadden, *Slave Patrols: Law and Violence in Virginia and the Carolinas* (Cambridge: Harvard University Press, 2001); Sylvia R. Frey, *Water from the Rock: Black Resistance in a Revolutionary Age* (Princeton: Princeton University Press, 1991); Sylvia R. Frey, "Between Slavery and Freedom: Virginia Blacks in the American Revolution," *Journal of Southern History* 49, no. 3 (August 1983): 375–98.

7. William Waller Hening, ed., *The Statutes at Large: Being a Collection of All the Laws of Virginia from the First Session of the Legislature, in the Year 1619*, 3 vols. (Philadelphia: Bartow, 1823), 447–63.

8. William L. Saunders, ed., *The Colonial Records of North Carolina, 1734–1752*, 4 vols. (Raleigh: Hale, 1886).

9. James Iredell, *Laws of the State of North Carolina* (Edenton, N.C.: Hodge and Wills, 1791–1800), 85–95.

10. Jeffrey J. Crow, "Slave Rebelliousness in North Carolina, 1775 to 1802," *William and Mary Quarterly* 37, no. 1 (January 1980): 79–102.

11. Marjoleine Kars, *Breaking Loose Together: The Regulator Rebellion in Pre-Revolutionary North Carolina* (Chapel Hill: University of North Carolina Press, 2002).

12. Woody Holton, *Forced Founders: Indians, Debtors, Slaves, and the Making of the American Revolution in Virginia* (Chapel Hill: University of North Carolina Press, 1999), xiv–xvii.

13. Alexander X. Byrd, *Captives and Voyagers: Black Migrants across the Eighteenth-Century British Atlantic World* (Baton Rouge: Louisiana State University Press, 2008); James Sidbury, *Becoming African in America: Race and Nation in the Early Black Atlantic* (New York: Oxford University Press, 2007), 80–81; Harvey Amani Whitfield,

Blacks on the Border: The Black Refugees in British North America, 1815–1860 (Burlington: University of Vermont Press, 2006).

CHAPTER 1. "LIV'D BY HIMSELF IN THE DESERT ABOUT 13 YEARS"

1. Carla Gardina Pestana, *The English Atlantic in an Age of Revolution, 1640–1661* (Cambridge: Harvard University Press, 2004); David Armitage, *The Ideological Origins of the British Empire* (Cambridge: Cambridge University Press, 2000); Linda Colley, *Britons: Forging the Nation, 1707–1837* (New Haven: Yale University Press, 1992).

2. Account Book of William Aitchison and James Parker, 1763–1804, 51–52, 84, Albert and Shirley Small Special Collections Library, University of Virginia, Charlottesville.

3. Ibid., 78.

4. Marisa J. Fuentes, *Dispossessed Lives: Enslaved Women, Violence, and the Archive* (Philadelphia: University of Pennsylvania Press, 2016).

5. Daina Ramey Berry, *The Price for a Pound of Their Flesh: The Value of the Enslaved, from Womb to Grave, in the Building of a Nation* (Boston: Beacon, 2017).

6. Account Book of Aitchison and Parker, 51.

7. On the burning of Norfolk, see Michael A. McDonnell, *The Politics of War: Race, Class, and Conflict in Revolutionary Virginia* (Chapel Hill: University of North Carolina Press, 2007), 169–70.

8. David S. Cecelski, *The Waterman's Song: Slavery and Freedom in Maritime North Carolina* (Chapel Hill: University of North Carolina Press, 2001), 109–16; Marvin L. Michael Kay and Lorin Lee Cary, *Slavery in North Carolina, 1748–1775* (Chapel Hill: University of North Carolina Press, 1995).

9. I thank Earl Ijames, curator of the African American Collection at the North Carolina Museum of History in Raleigh, for this perspective.

10. Bradford J. Wood and Larry E. Tise, "The Conundrum of Unfree Labor," in *New Voyages to Carolina: Reinterpreting North Carolina History*, ed. Larry E. Tise and Jeffrey J. Crow (Chapel Hill: University of North Carolina Press, 2017), 85–109; Bradford J. Wood, *This Remote Part of the World: Regional Formation in the Lower Cape Fear, North Carolina, 1725–1775* (Columbia: University of South Carolina Press, 2004); Kay and Cary, *Slavery in North Carolina*.

As North Carolina's population expanded, the capital was moved to more central locations—New Bern in 1770 and then Raleigh, established in 1792. See Stanley R. Riggs and Dorothea V. Ames, "An Uncompromising Environment: North Carolina's 'Land of Water' Coastal System," in *New Voyages to Carolina*, ed. Tise and Crow, 14–40; Michael Leroy Oberg and David Moore, "Voyages to Carolina: Europeans in the Indians' Old World," in *New Voyages to Carolina*, ed. Tise and Crow, 41–59; Stephen Feeley, "Intercolonial Conflict and Cooperation during the Tuscarora War," in *New Voyages to Carolina*, ed. Tise and Crow, 60–84.

11. Charles Royster, *The Fabulous History of the Dismal Swamp Land Company: A Story of George Washington's Times* (New York: Vintage, 1999), 81–82.

12. Evidence of the Dismal Swamp Company's incorporation passed among the networks of Virginia and North Carolina's land speculators soon after the company formed. See Samuel Johnston to Thomas Barker, April 1763, Hayes Collection #324, Southern Historical Collection, Wilson Library, University of North Carolina at Chapel Hill; Articles of Agreement, Dismal Swamp Land Company, November 3, 1763, in *The Papers of George Washington*, Colonial Series, vol. 7, January 1761–June 1767, ed. W. W. Abbot and Dorothy Twohig (Charlottesville: University Press of Virginia, 1990, 271–73; Royster, *Fabulous History*, 81.

13. Royster, *Fabulous History*, 83–87, 97–98.

14. Ibid., 98–99.

15. *Virginia Gazette*, June 23, October 6, 1768, April 13, 1769; Daniel O. Sayers, *A Desolate Place for a Defiant People: The Archaeology of Maroons, Indigenous Americans, and Enslaved Laborers in the Great Dismal Swamp* (Gainesville: University Press of Florida, 2014), 88–89; Ted Maris-Wolf, "Between Slavery and Freedom: African Americans in the Great Dismal Swamp, 1763–1861" (master's thesis, College of William and Mary, 2002); Lathan A. Windley, *A Profile of Runaway Slaves in Virginia and South Carolina from 1730–1787* (New York: Garland, 1995), 287, 291–92; Tom Costa, *The Geography of Slavery in Virginia Digital Project* (Charlottesville: Rectors and Visitors of the University of Virginia, 2005). On country marks, see Michael A. Gomez, *Exchanging Our Country Marks: The Transformation of African Identities in the Colonial and Antebellum South* (Chapel Hill: University of North Carolina Press, 1998).

16. Sayers, *Desolate Place*, 89.

17. Royster, *Fabulous History*, 88, 155–56.

18. John Ferdinand Dalziel Smyth, *A Tour in the United States of America*, 2 vols. (Dublin: Price, Moncrieffe, 1784), 102; Sayers, *Desolate Place*, 89.

19. David Jameson to John Driver, December 5, 1783, letter copy, DSLC Records, box 1, folder 2.

20. Ibid.

21. John Driver to David Jameson, January 15, 1790, in ibid.

22. Thomas Walker to David Jameson, June 23, 1783, in ibid.

23. Ibid., June 26, 1783.

24. David Jameson to John Page, John Lewis, and Thomas Newton, October 21, 1783, letter copy, in ibid.

25. Robert Andrews to David Jameson, December 27, 1783, in ibid.

26. David Jameson to David Meade, April 1784, in ibid.

27. Royster, *Fabulous History*, 312.

28. David Jameson to William Nelson, January 4, 1785, David Jameson to J. Collee, February 1785, letter copy, both in DSLC Records, box 1, folder 2.

29. Royster, *Fabulous History*, 313.

30. John Driver to David Jameson, August 26, 1786, DSLC Records, box 1, folder 2.

31. David Jameson to John Driver, January 25, 1787, letter copy, in ibid.

32. John Driver to David Jameson, February 25, 1787, in ibid.

33. Ibid., June 13, 1787.

34. Ibid., October 1, 1787.

35. Ibid., February 11, 1788.
36. Ibid., May 15, 1788.
37. Ibid., June 6, 1788.
38. Ibid., June 2, 1788.
39. Ibid., January 8, 1789.
40. Ibid., June 10, 1789.
41. Ibid.
42. Ibid., June 17, 1789.
43. Ibid., July 6, 1789.
44. Ibid., August 17, 1789.
45. Ibid., September 5, 1789.
46. Ibid., September 24, 1789.
47. Ibid., December 7, 1789.
48. Ibid., January 15, 1790.
49. Ibid., May 2, 1790.
50. Ibid., August 3, 1790.
51. Ibid., February 25, 1791.
52. Joseph Hornsby to David Jameson, January 20, 1790, in ibid.
53. John Driver to David Jameson, July 11, 1791, in ibid.
54. Ibid.

CHAPTER 2. "LAWLESS SETTE OF VILLAINS"

1. Ada Ferrer, *Freedom's Mirror: Cuba and Haiti in the Age of Revolution* (New York: Cambridge University Press, 2014); Gordon S. Brown, *Toussaint's Clause: The Founding Fathers and the Haitian Revolution* (Jackson: University Press of Mississippi, 2005); Laurent Dubois, *Avengers of the New World: The Story of the Haitian Revolution* (Cambridge: Belknap Press of Harvard University Press, 2004); Laurent Dubois, *A Colony of Citizens: Revolution and Slave Emancipation in the French Caribbean, 1787–1804* (Chapel Hill: University of North Carolina Press, 2004); Carolyn E. Fick, *The Making of Haiti: The Saint Domingue Revolution from Below* (Knoxville: University of Tennessee Press, 1990).

2. *Wilmington City Gazette*, July 18, 1795; also quoted in Herbert Aptheker, *American Negro Slave Revolts: On Nat Turner, Denmark Vesey, Gabriel, and Others*, 50th anniv. ed. (New York: International, 1993), 217.

3. Michael Sivapragasam, "After the Treaties: A Social, Economic and Demographic History of Maroon Society in Jamaica, 1739–1842" (PhD diss., University of Southampton, 2018), 144–47; Daive A. Dunkley, *Agency of the Enslaved: Jamaica and the Culture of Freedom in the Atlantic World* (Lanham, Md.: Lexington Books, 2013); Kenneth M. Bilby, *True-Born Maroons* (Gainesville: University Press of Florida, 2005); Karla Gotlieb, *A History of Queen Nanny: Leader of the Windward Maroons* (Trenton, N.J.: Africa World, 2000); Bev Carey, *The Maroon Story: The Authentic and Original History of the Maroons in the History of Jamaica, 1490–1880* (St. Andrew, Jamaica: Agouti, 1997); Mavis C. Campbell, *The Maroons of Jamaica, 1655–1796: A History of Resistance, Collaboration, and Betrayal* (Granby, Mass.: Bergin and Garvey,

1988); Michael Craton, *Testing the Chains: Resistance to Slavery in the British West Indies* (Ithaca: Cornell University Press, 1982).

4. *State Gazette of North Carolina*, March 2, 30, 1793, in *Stealing a Little Freedom: Slave Runaway Advertisements in North Carolina, 1791–1840*, ed. Freddie L. Parker (New York: Garland, 1994), 21–22.

5. *North-Carolina Gazette, or Impartial Intelligencer and Weekly Advertiser*, March 23, 1793, in *Stealing a Little Freedom*, ed. Parker, 4; Michael J. Jarvis, *In the Eye of All Trade: Bermuda, Bermudians, and the Maritime Atlantic World, 1680–1783* (Chapel Hill: University of North Carolina Press, 2010); Charles R. Foy, "Seeking Freedom in the Atlantic World, 1713–1783," *Early American Studies* 4, no. 1 (Spring 2006): 46–77; David S. Cecelski, *The Waterman's Song: Slavery and Freedom in Maritime North Carolina* (Chapel Hill: University of North Carolina Press, 2001); Peter Linebaugh and Marcus Rediker, *The Many-Headed Hydra: Sailors, Slaves, Commoners, and the Hidden History of the Revolutionary Atlantic* (Boston: Beacon, 2000); W. Jeffrey Bolster, *Black Jacks: African American Seamen in the Age of Sail* (Cambridge: Harvard University Press, 1997).

6. Cecelski, *Waterman's Song*; Dorothy Spruill Redford, *Somerset Homecoming: Recovering a Lost Heritage* (Chapel Hill: University of North Carolina Press, 2000).

7. John Hope Franklin and Loren Schweninger, *Runaway Slaves: Rebels on the Plantation* (New York: Oxford University Press, 1999); Lathan A. Windley, ed., *A Profile of Runaway Slaves in Virginia and South Carolina from 1730–1787* (New York: Garland, 1995); Freddie L. Parker, ed., *Running for Freedom: Slave Runaways in North Carolina, 1775–1840* (New York: Garland, 1993).

8. Bradford J. Wood and Larry E. Tise, "The Conundrum of Unfree Labor," in *New Voyages to Carolina: Reinterpreting North Carolina History*, ed. Larry E. Tise and Jeffrey J. Crow (Chapel Hill: University of North Carolina Press, 2017), 85–109. See also William L. Byrd III, *North Carolina Slaves and Free Persons of Color: Pasquotank County* (Westminster, Md.: Heritage, 2006); William L. Byrd III, *North Carolina Slaves and Free Persons of Color: Perquimans County* (Westminster, Md.: Heritage, 2005).

9. I borrow the term "geography of resistance" from Stephanie M. H. Camp, *Closer to Freedom: Enslaved Women and Everyday Resistance in the Plantation South* (Chapel Hill: University of North Carolina Press, 2004).

10. Jared Ross Hardesty, *Unfreedom: Slavery and Dependence in Eighteenth-Century Boston* (New York: New York University Press, 2016); Wendy Warren, *New England Bound: Slavery and Colonization in Early America* (New York: Liveright, 2016); Margaret Ellen Newell, *Brethren by Nature: New England Indians, Colonists, and the Origins of American Slavery* (Ithaca: Cornell University Press, 2015); Christopher Cameron, *To Plead Our Own Cause: African Americans in Massachusetts and the Making of the Antislavery Movement* (Kent, Ohio: Kent State University Press, 2014); Emily Blanck, *Tyrannicide: Forging an American Law of Slavery in Revolutionary South Carolina and Massachusetts* (Athens: University of Georgia Press, 2014); Margot Minardi, *Making Slavery History: Abolitionism and the Politics of Memory in Massachu-*

setts (New York: Oxford University Press, 2012); Catherine Adams and Elizabeth H. Pleck, *Love of Freedom: Black Women in Colonial and Revolutionary New England* (New York: Oxford University Press, 2010); Joanne Pope Melish, *Disowning Slavery: Gradual Emancipation and "Race" in New England, 1780–1860* (Ithaca: Cornell University Press, 1998); William D. Pierson, *Black Yankees: The Development of an Afro-American Subculture in Eighteenth-Century New England* (Amherst: University of Massachusetts Press, 1988).

11. Christy Clark-Pujara, *Dark Work: The Business of Slavery in Rhode Island* (New York: New York University Press, 2016); Kenneth E. Marshall, *Manhood Enslaved: Bondmen in Eighteenth and Early Nineteenth Century New Jersey* (Rochester, N.Y.: University of Rochester Press, 2011); Leslie M. Alexander, *African or American? Black Identity and Political Activism in New York City, 1784–1861* (Urbana: University of Illinois Press, 2008); Leslie M. Harris, *In the Shadow of Slavery: African Americans in New York City, 1626–1863* (Chicago: University of Chicago Press, 2003); Milton C. Sernett, *North Star Country: Upstate New York and the Crusade for African American Freedom* (Syracuse: Syracuse University Press, 2001); Graham Russell Hodges, *Root and Branch: African Americans in New York and East Jersey, 1613–1863* (Chapel Hill: University of North Carolina Press, 1999).

12. Eva Sheppard Wolf, *Almost Free: A Story about Family and Race in Antebellum Virginia* (Athens: University of Georgia Press, 2012); Eva Sheppard Wolf, *Race and Liberty in the New Nation: Emancipation in Virginia from the Revolution to Nat Turner's Rebellion* (Baton Rouge: Louisiana State University Press, 2006); Douglas R. Egerton, *Death or Liberty: African Americans and Revolutionary America* (New York: Oxford University Press, 2009); Melvin Patrick Ely, *Israel on the Appomattox: A Southern Experiment in Black Freedom from the 1790s through the Civil War* (New York: Vintage, 2004); Dylan Penningroth, *Claims of Kinfolk: African American Property and Community in the Nineteenth-Century South* (Chapel Hill: University of North Carolina Press, 2003); James Sidbury, *Becoming African in America: Race and Nation in the Early Black Atlantic* (New York: Oxford University Press, 2007); James Sidbury, *Ploughshares into Swords: Race, Rebellion, and Identity in Gabriel's Virginia, 1730–1810* (New York: Cambridge University Press, 1997); Barbara Jeanne Fields, *Slavery and Freedom on the Middle Ground: Maryland during the Nineteenth Century* (New Haven: Yale University Press, 1985).

13. Richard Follett, *The Sugar Masters: Planters and Slaves in Louisiana's Cane World, 1820–1860* (Baton Rouge: Louisiana State University Press, 2007); Thomas N. Ingersoll, *Mammon and Manon in Early New Orleans: The First Slave Society in the Deep South, 1718–1819* (Knoxville: University of Tennessee Press, 1999); Leslie A. Schwalm, *A Hard Fight for We: Women's Transition from Slavery to Freedom in South Carolina* (Urbana: University of Illinois Press, 1997).

14. Thomas Shepherd to William Nelson and John Jameson, August 17, 1798, DSLC Records, box 1, folder 2.

15. Thomas Shepherd to John Jameson, September 14, 1798, in ibid.

16. Ibid., November 28, 1798.

17. Ibid.

18. Thomas Shepherd to John Brown, January 13, 1799, in ibid.

19. Thomas Shepherd to John Brown, April 11, August 29, 1799, both in ibid.

20. Thomas Shepherd to William Nelson, January 6, 1800, in ibid.

21. Ibid., February 27, 1800.

22. Ibid., March 23, 1800.

23. Ibid.

24. Charles Royster, *The Fabulous History of the Dismal Swamp Land Company: A Story of George Washington's Times* (New York: Vintage, 1999), 393.

25. Thomas Shepherd to Thomas Swepson, May 16, 1800, DSLC Records, box 1, folder 2.

26. Thomas Shepherd to William Nelson, June 14, 1800, in ibid.

27. Thomas Swepson to William Nelson, July 20, 1800, in ibid. For the enclosed letter, see Shepherd to Swepson (no. 2), May 12, 1800, DSLC Records, box 1, folder 2.

28. Thomas Shepherd to William Nelson, August 17, 1800, DSLC Records, box 1, folder 2.

29. William Nelson Jr. to Thomas Swepson, October 8, 1800, in ibid.

30. Dismal Swamp Company manager meeting notes, January 1801, in ibid.

31. Ibid., June 30, 1801.

32. Thomas Shepherd to Corbin Griffin, July 31, 1801, in ibid.

33. Douglas R. Egerton, *Gabriel's Rebellion: The Virginia Slave Conspiracies of 1800 and 1802* (Chapel Hill: University of North Carolina Press, 1993), ix.

34. Philip D. Morgan, "Conspiracy Scares," *William and Mary Quarterly* 59, no. 1 (January 2002): 159–66; Sidbury, *Ploughshares into Swords*.

35. Second confession of Jesse Blackwood, June 27, 1822, in Lionel H. Kennedy and Thomas Parker, *An Official Report of the Trials of Sundry Negroes, Charged with an Attempt to Raise an Insurrection in the State of South-Carolina* (Charleston: Schenck, 1822); Egerton, *Gabriel's Conspiracy*, 125.

36. Testimony of Smith's Robin at the trial of Smith's Abram, May 1, 1802, testimony of Smith's Abram at trial of Booker's Sancho, April 23, 1802, testimony of Smith's Abram at trial of Robertson's Frank, April 23, 1802, all in Monroe Papers; Egerton, *Gabriel's Conspiracy*, 124; Rhys Isaac, *The Transformation of Virginia, 1740–1790* (Chapel Hill: University of North Carolina Press, 1982), 103.

37. Testimony of Smith's Robin at trial of Smith's Abram, May 1, 1802, John B. Scott to James Monroe, April 21, 1802, testimony of Sandifer's Bob at trial of Booker's Sancho, April 23, 1802, all in Monroe Papers; testimony of Ned at trial of Hillard's Absalom, April 26, 1802, all in Halifax County Court Order Book, LV; sentence of Booker's Sancho, April 23, 1802, in Condemned Slaves 1802, Executed, Auditor's Item 153, box 2, LV; Egerton, *Gabriel's Conspiracy*, 124–26.

38. Testimony of Green's Ned at trial of Royall's Bob, January 7, 1802, testimony of Jones's Hampton at trial of Jones's Joe, January 7, 1802, both in in Monroe Papers; Bogger, *Free Blacks in Norfolk, Virginia*, 1–5; Egerton, *Gabriel's Conspiracy*, 126–27.

39. Testimony of Jackson's Adam, Jackson's George, Wilkes's Jeffrey, and Jackson's

Raysom at trial of Wilkes's Isaac, February 11, 1802, all in Monroe Papers; Egerton, *Gabriel's Conspiracy*, 128–31.

40. William Prentis to James Monroe, January 5, 1802, testimony of Willis Pillar at trial of Jones's Joe, January 7, 1802, William Martin to James Monroe, January 2, 1802, Richard Jones to William Prentis, January 2, 1802, William Prentis to James Monroe, January 4, 1802, James Monroe to General Assembly, January 16, 1802, all in Monroe Papers; Egerton, *Gabriel's Conspiracy*, 132–33.

41. Testimony of Jackson's George, Jackson's Adam, and Wilkes's Jeffrey at trial of Wilkes's Isaac, February 3, 1802, sentence of Wilkes's Isaac, February 3, 1802, sentence of Hagood's Phill, February 3, 1802, certification of death for Isaac, signed by James Rice and John Tucker, September 13, 1802, all in Condemned Slaves 1802, Executed, Auditor's Item 153, box 2, LV; John Cowper to James Monroe, April 17, 1802, testimony of Caleb Boush at trial of Ingram's Ned, June 20, 1802, both in Monroe Papers; testimony of Walke's Will at trial of Ingram's Ned, June 20, 1802, testimony of John Floyd at trial of Ingram's Ned, June 20, 1802, both in Norfolk County Court Order Book, LV; Egerton, *Gabriel's Conspiracy*, 134–36.

42. Testimony of Smith's Abram and Sandifer's Bob at trial of Booker's Sancho, April 23, 1802, sentence of Hilliard's Absalom, April 26, 1802, sentence of Robertson's Frank, April 23, 1802, sentence of Bass's Martin, April 26, 1802, sentence of Smith's Abram, May 1, 1802, all in Halifax County Court Order Book, LV; sentence of Booker's Sancho, April 23, 1802, certification of death for Booker's Sancho, signed by John Wimbish, May 15, 1802, certification of death for Hilliard's Absalom, signed by John Wimbish, June 4, 1802, certification of death for Bass's Martin, signed by John Wimbish, July 6, 1802, certification of death for Robertson's Frank, signed by John Wimbish, July 6, 1802, certification of death for Smith's Abram, signed by John Wimbish, July 6, 1802, all in Condemned Slaves 1802, Executed, Auditor's Item 153, box 2, LV; testimony of Sandifer's Bob at trial of Smith's Abram, May 1, 1802, John Scott to James Monroe, April 30, 1802, both in Monroe Papers; Egerton, *Gabriel's Conspiracy*, 139–41.

43. William R. Davie to Benjamin Williams, February 17, 1802, Historical Society of Pennsylvania Papers, 1760–1888, SANC; deposition of Fitt's Dennis, June 15, 1802, Slave Collection, 1784–1856, SANC; *Raleigh Register and North Carolina Gazette*, July 6, 1802; *Virginia Herald*, June 29, 1802; Egerton, *Gabriel's Conspiracy*, 143–46.

44. Egerton, *Gabriel's Conspiracy*, 121–22; Douglas R. Egerton, "'Fly across the River': The Easter Slave Conspiracy of 1802," *North Carolina Historical Review* 68, no. 2 (April 1991): 88.

45. Cecelski, *Waterman's Song*, 129.

CHAPTER 3. "ALL DELINQUENTS IN DUTY"

1. Richard Blow to George Blow and Alexander Scammell, July 29, 1801, RBL, 1801–3.

2. Ibid., October 28, 1807, RBL, 1807–9.

3. Charles Royster, *The Fabulous History of the Dismal Swamp Company: A Story of*

George Washington's Times (New York: Vintage, 1999); David S. Cecelski, *The Waterman's Song: Slavery and Freedom in Maritime North Carolina* (Chapel Hill: University of North Carolina Press, 2001), 105–9; Peter Way, *Common Labour: Workers and the Digging of North American Canals, 1780–1860* (New York: Cambridge University Press, 1993), 21.

4. Richard Blow to Colonel Thomas Newton, January 7, 1806, RBL, 1806.

5. Richard Blow to Richard S. Green, January 21, 1806, in ibid.

6. Richard Blow to Samuel Proctor, January 21, 1806, in ibid.

7. Ibid.

8. Ibid.

9. Ibid., January 23, 1807, RBL, 1807–9.

10. Ibid., May 29, 1807.

11. Ibid., June 2, 1807.

12. Ibid., July 3, 1808.

13. See Loren Schweninger, "The Underside of Slavery: The Internal Economy, Self-Hire, and Quasi-Freedom in Virginia, 1780–1865," *Slavery and Abolition* 12, no. 2 (1991): 1–22.

14. Richard Blow to Samuel Proctor, December 6, 1808, RBL, 1807–9.

15. Alan Kulikoff, *Tobacco and Slaves: The Development of Southern Cultures in the Chesapeake, 1680–1800* (Chapel Hill: University of North Carolina Press, 1986); Lorena S. Walsh, "Slave Life, Slave Society, and Tobacco Production in the Tidewater Chesapeake, 1620–1820," in *Cultivation and Culture: Labor and the Shaping of Slave Life in the Americas*, ed. Ira Berlin and Philip D. Morgan (Charlottesville: University Press of Virginia, 1993), 170–99; Ira Berlin, *Many Thousands Gone* (Cambridge: Belknap Press of Harvard University Press, 1998), 134–35; Peter Kolchin, *American Slavery, 1619–1877* (New York: Hill and Wang, 2003), 24–33.

16. Samuel Proctor to James Henderson, March 12, 1816, DSLC Records, box 1, folder 2.

17. Ibid., March 19, 1816.

18. Samuel Proctor to the Dismal Swamp Land Company, June 31, 1817, DSLC Records, box 1, folder 2.

19. Samuel Proctor to James Henderson, August 15, 1818, in ibid.

20. Samuel Proctor to the Dismal Swamp Land Company, January 11, 1819, DSLC Records, box 1, folder 2.

21. Samuel Proctor to Thomas Griffin, December 12, 1820, DSLC Records, box 1, folder 2.

22. Ibid., December 1820.

23. Drew R. McCoy, *The Elusive Republic: Political Economy in Jeffersonian America* (Chapel Hill: University of North Carolina Press, 1980), 209–35; Burton Spivak, *Jefferson's English Crisis: Commerce, Embargo, and the Republican Revolution* (Charlottesville: University of Virginia Press, 1988); Alan Taylor, *The Internal Enemy: Slavery and War in Virginia, 1772–1832* (New York: Norton, 2013), 130–31.

24. Pronounced in March, Samuel Proctor's will was entered into the county will

book in May 1831 (Will Book C, Camden County, North Carolina, May 1831, 123–25, SANC).

CHAPTER 4. "TO MANAGE THE BUSINESS OF THE SWAMP"

1. Moses Grandy, "Narrative of the Life of Moses Grandy," in *North Carolina Slave Narratives: The Lives of Moses Roper, Lunsford Lane, Moses Grandy, and Thomas H. Jones*, ed. William L. Andrews (Chapel Hill: University of North Carolina Press, 2003), 23–78; notes on the publication of Grandy's narrative are drawn from Andreá N. Williams's introduction, 146–48. See also Calvin Schermerhorn, *Money over Mastery, Family over Freedom: Slavery in the Antebellum Upper South* (Baltimore: Johns Hopkins University Press, 2011): 64–79; Ted Maris-Wolf, "Hidden in Plain Sight: Maroon Life and Labor in Virginia's Dismal Swamp," *Slavery and Abolition* 34, no. 3 (2013): 446–64.

2. Annette Gordon-Reed and Peter S. Onuf, *"Most Blessed of the Patriarchs": Thomas Jefferson and the Empire of the Imagination* (New York: Norton, 2016); Annette Gordon-Reed, *The Hemingses of Monticello: An American Family* (New York: Norton, 2008); Lucia Stanton, *"Those Who Labor for My Happiness": Slavery at Thomas Jefferson's Monticello* (Charlottesville: University of Virginia Press, 2012).

3. Joshua M. Smith, *Borderland Smuggling: Patriots, Loyalists, and Illicit Trade in the Northeast, 1783–1820* (Gainesville: University Press of Florida, 2006); Jeffrey A. Frankel, "The 1807–1809 Embargo against Great Britain," *Journal of Economic History* 42, no. 2 (June 1982): 291–308.

4. Grandy, "Narrative," 170–71.

5. Mechal Sobel, *Teach Me Dreams: The Search for Self in the Revolutionary Era* (Princeton: Princeton University Press, 2002), 127–28.

6. Frederick Hall to James Henderson, February 3, 1815, DSLC Papers, 1814–16, box 2, c. 1.

7. Ibid., January 11, 1816.

8. Ibid.

9. Thomas Swepson to James Henderson, January 17, 1816, in ibid.

10. Ibid., February 8, 1816.

11. Ibid., March 22, 1816.

12. Edwin Sexton to James Henderson, February 3, 1816, in ibid.

13. Matthew Spencer and Stephen Spencer to James Henderson, March 6, 1816, in ibid.

14. Ibid., March 29, 1816.

15. Thomas Swepson to James Henderson, January 14, 1817, in ibid.

16. Thomas Griffin to James Henderson, December 22, 1817, in ibid.

17. David Meade to James Henderson, January 15, 1817, in ibid.

18. Frederick Hall to James Henderson, February 17, 1816, in ibid.

19. Ibid., March 14, 1816.

20. Ibid., March 23, 1816.

21. Ibid., April 16, 1816.

22. Ibid., June 29, 1816.

23. Ibid., November 22, 1816.

24. Ibid., January 18, 1817, DSLC Records, box 1, folder 2.

25. Ibid., March 15, 1817.

26. Ibid., April 17, 1817.

27. Ibid., June 30, 1817.

28. Ibid., August 24, 1817.

29. Ibid., November 17, 1817.

30. Ibid., January 16, 1818.

31. Ibid.

32. Ibid., March 10, 1818.

33. Ibid., March 20, 1818.

34. Ibid., August 29, 1818.

35. Ibid., October 27, 1818.

36. Ibid., December 8, 1818.

37. Frederick Hall to Thomas B. Griffin, December 28, 1818, in ibid.

38. Ibid., January 22, 1819, DSLC Records, box 1, folder 2.

39. Ibid., February 20, 1819.

40. Ibid., October 26, 1819.

41. Ibid., April 17, 1820.

42. Ibid., June 30, 1820.

43. "Notes on Jericho Mill 1820, the Bill for F. Hall, AG of the D.S. Land Company," May 13, 1820, in ibid.

CHAPTER 5. "INTENTION OF THE NEGROES WAS TO REACH THE DISMAL SWAMP"

1. *Daily National Intelligencer*, August 29, 1831.

2. Ibid.; *Richmond Constitutional Whig*, August 29, 1831.

3. David F. Allmendinger Jr., *Nat Turner and the Rising in Southampton County* (Baltimore: Johns Hopkins University Press, 2014), 1–8.

4. Peter H. Wood, "Nat Turner: The Unknown Slave as Visionary Leader," in *Black Leaders of the Nineteenth Century*, ed. Leon Litwack and August Meier (Urbana: University of Illinois Press, 1988), 27–40; Charles Edward Morris, "Panic and Reprisal: Reaction in North Carolina to the Nat Turner Insurrection, 1831," *North Carolina Historical Review* 62, no. 1 (January 1985): 29–52.

5. James O'Neil Spady, "Power and Confession: On the Credibility of the Earliest Reports of the Denmark Vesey Slave Conspiracy," *William and Mary Quarterly* 68, no. 2 (2011): 287–304; James Sidbury, "Reading, Revelation, and Rebellion: The Textual Communities of Gabriel, Denmark Vesey, and Nat Turner," in *Nat Turner*, ed. Greenberg, 119–33; Douglas R. Egerton, *He Shall Go Out Free: The Lives of Denmark Vesey* (Madison, Wis.: Madison House, 1999).

6. Allmendinger, *Nat Turner*, 1–8.

7. Greenberg, *Nat Turner*; Stephen B. Oates, *The Fires of Jubilee: Nat Turner's Fierce Rebellion* (New York: New American Library, 1975); Henry Irving Tragle, ed., *The*

Southampton Slave Revolt of 1831: A Compilation of Source Material Including the Full Text of the "Confessions" of Nat Turner (New York: Vintage, 1973).

8. Manisha Sinha, *The Slave's Cause: A History of Abolition* (New Haven: Yale University Press, 2016); Benjamin Quarles, *Black Abolitionists* (New York: Oxford University Press, 1969).

9. William G. Shade, *Democratizing the Old Dominion: Virginia and the Second Party System, 1824–1861* (Charlottesville: University of Virginia Press, 1996).

10. Eva Sheppard Wolf, *Race and Liberty in the New Nation: Emancipation in Virginia from the Revolution to Nat Turner's Rebellion* (Baton Rouge: Louisiana State University Press, 2006).

11. Bradford J. Wood and Larry E. Tise, "The Conundrum of Unfree Labor," in *New Voyages to Carolina: Reinterpreting North Carolina History,* ed. Larry E. Tise and Jeffrey J. Crow (Chapel Hill: University of North Carolina Press, 2017), 85–109.

12. Edmund Ruffin, "Observations Made during an Excursion to the Dismal Swamp," *Farmer's Register* 4, no. 9 (January 1837): 513–21. On Ruffin, see David F. Allmendinger, *Ruffin: Family and Reform in the Old South* (New York: Oxford University Press, 1990); William M. Mathew, *Edmund Ruffin and the Crisis of Slavery in the Old South: The Failure of Agricultural Reform* (Athens: University of Georgia Press, 1988); Betty L. Mitchell, *Edmund Ruffin: A Biography* (Bloomington: Indiana University Press, 1981).

13. Josiah Riddick to William Shepherd, December 15, 1832, DSLC Records, box 1, folder 5.

14. William Shepherd to Josiah Riddick, December 18, 1832, in ibid.

15. Kyle and Paul to William Shepherd, Receipt of Payment, October 12, 1833, in ibid.

16. William Shepherd to Jesse Perry, Account List, October 25, 1833, in ibid.

17. William Shepherd, "First Quarter Returns," February 3, 1835, "Second Quarter Returns," n.d., both in ibid.

18. William Shepherd, "February Report," March 1, 1834, in ibid.

19. William Shepherd, "March Report," March 31, 1834, in ibid.

20. William Shepherd, "April Report," April 20, 1834, in ibid.

21. William Shepherd, "May Report," May 1834, "September Report," October 1, 1834, both in ibid.

22. William Shepherd, "May Report," June 1, 1835, William Shepherd, "October Report," November 1, 1835, both in ibid.

23. William Shepherd, "December Report," January 1, 1834, in ibid.

24. William Shepherd, "May Report," June 1, 1835, in ibid.; David S. Cecelski, *The Waterman's Song: Slavery and Freedom in Maritime North Carolina* (Chapel Hill: University of North Carolina Press, 2001); Dorothy Spruill Redford, *Somerset Homecoming: Recovering a Lost Heritage* (Chapel Hill: University of North Carolina Press, 2000).

25. William Shepherd to Sewellin Jones, $60 Slave Hire Receipt, January 1, 1833, DSLC Records, box 1, folder 5.

26. Ibid.; $100 Slave Hire Receipt, January 1, 1835, DSLC Records, box 1, folder 5.

27. William Shepherd to Jacob Keeling, $65 Slave Hire Receipt, January 1, 1835, in ibid.

28. Ibid.; $90 Slave Hire Receipt, January 1, 1835, DSLC Records, box 1, folder 5.

29. William Shepherd to John S. Denson, $30 Slave Hire Receipt, January 1, 1835, in ibid.

30. Joseph Holladay, "Third Quarter Report," "November 1836 Report," both in DSLC Records, box 1, folder 7.

31. Joseph Holladay to Robert Butler, February 20, 1836, in ibid.

32. Ibid., May 26, 1836.

33. Joseph Holladay, "June Report," June 30, 1836, in ibid.

34. Joseph Holladay receipt, October 26, 1836, in ibid.

35. Jessica M. Lepler, *The Many Panics of 1837: People, Politics, and the Creation of a Transatlantic Financial Crisis* (New York: Cambridge University Press, 2013).

36. Joseph Holladay, "First Quarter Report," February 1, 1838, "February Report," March 1, 1838, "March Report," April 1, 1838, all in DSLC Records, box 1, folder 9.

37. Joseph Holladay, "Second Quarter Report," May 1, 1838, "May Report," June 1, 1838, "June Report," June 30, 1838, "Third Quarter Report," July 31, 1838, "First Quarter Report," February 1, 1838, all in DSLC Records, box 1, folders 9, 11.

38. Joseph Holladay to Robert Butler, January 1, 1836, in ibid., box 1, folder 7.

39. Joseph Holladay to Robert Rogers, $20.25 Slave Hire Receipt, December 27, 1844, Joseph Holladay to John C. Cahoon, $40 Slave Hire Receipt, January 1, 1845, Joseph Holladay to Elisha Norfleet, $25 Slave Hire Receipt, January 1, 1845, Joseph Holladay to Caty Copeland, $25 Slave Hire Receipt, January 1, 1845, all in ibid., box 2, folder 18; Joseph Holladay to Henry Rawls, $102 Slave Hire Receipt, January 1, 1848, DSLC Records, box 2, folder 17.

CHAPTER 6. "SLAVES IN THE DISMAL SWAMP"

1. Frederick Douglass, "Slaves in the Dismal Swamp," *North Star*, March 31, 1848.

2. Ibid.

3. John Lauritz Larson, *The Market Revolution in America: Liberty, Ambition, and the Eclipse of the Common Good* (New York: Cambridge University Press, 2010); T. H. Breen, *Marketplace of Revolution: How Consumer Politics Shaped American Independence* (New York: Oxford University Press, 2004); T. H. Breen, "'Baubles of Britain': The American and Consumer Revolutions of the Eighteenth Century," *Past and Present* 119, no. 1 (May 1988): 73–104; Melvyn Stokes and Stephen Conway, eds., *The Market Revolution in America* (Charlottesville: University Press of Virginia, 1996); Charles Sellers, *The Market Revolution: Jacksonian America, 1815–1846* (New York: Oxford University Press, 1991); Stuart M. Blumin, *The Emergence of the Middle Class: Social Experience in the American City, 1760–1900* (New York: Cambridge University Press, 1989).

4. John A. Muscalus, *The Dismal Swamp Canal and Lake Drummond Hotel on Paper Money, 1838–1865* (Bridgeport, Pa.: Historical Paper Money Research Institute, 1965); Jesse F. Pugh and Frank T. Williams, *The Hotel in the Great Dismal Swamp and Contemporary Events Thereabouts* (Old Trap, N.C.: Pugh, 1964).

5. Manisha Sinha, *The Slave's Cause: A History of Abolition* (New Haven: Yale University Press, 2016); Patrick Rael, *Eighty-Eight Years: The Long Death of Slavery in the United States, 1777–1865* (Athens: University of Georgia Press, 2015); Patrick Rael, *Black Identity and Black Protest in the Antebellum North* (Chapel Hill: University of North Carolina Press, 2002); Maurice Jackson, *Let This Voice Be Heard: Anthony Benezet, Father of Atlantic Abolitionism* (Philadelphia: University of Pennsylvania Press, 2009); Christopher Leslie Brown, *Moral Capital: Foundations of British Abolitionism* (Chapel Hill: University of North Carolina Press, 2006); Richard S. Newman, *The Transformation of American Abolitionism: Fighting Slavery in the Early Republic* (Chapel Hill: University of North Carolina Press, 2002); Peter P. Hinks, *To Awaken My Afflicted Brethren: David Walker and the Problem of Antebellum Slave Resistance* (University Park: Pennsylvania State University Press, 1997).

On David Walker's searing critique of American republican government, see David Walker, *Walker's Appeal, in Four Articles*, 3rd ed. (Boston, 1830), 82.

6. Andrew K. Diemer, *The Politics of Black Citizenship: Free African Americans in the Mid-Atlantic Borderland, 1817–1863* (Athens: University of Georgia Press, 2016); Elise Lemire, *Black Walden: Slavery and Its Aftermath in Concord, Massachusetts* (Philadelphia: University of Pennsylvania Press, 2009); Leslie M. Alexander, *African or American?: Black Identity and Political Activism in New York City, 1784–1861* (Urbana: University of Illinois Press, 2008); Leslie M. Harris, *In the Shadow of Slavery: African Americans in New York City, 1626–1863* (Chicago: University of Chicago Press, 2003); James Oliver Horton and Lois E. Horton, *In Hope of Liberty: Culture, Community, and Protest among Northern Free Blacks, 1700–1860* (New York: Oxford University Press, 1997); Christopher Phillips, *Freedom's Port: The African American Community of Baltimore, 1790–1860* (Urbana: University of Illinois Press, 1997); Gary B. Nash, *Forging Freedom: The Formation of Philadelphia's Black Community, 1720–1840* (Cambridge: Harvard University Press, 1988).

7. Bradford J. Wood and Larry E. Tise, "The Conundrum of Unfree Labor," in *New Voyages to Carolina: Reinterpreting North Carolina History*, ed. Larry E. Tise and Jeffrey J. Crow (Chapel Hill: University of North Carolina Press, 2017), 102.

8. James Oakes, *The Scorpion's Sting: Antislavery and the Coming of the Civil War* (New York: Norton, 2014); W. Caleb McDaniel, *The Problem of Democracy in the Age of Slavery: Garrisonian Abolitionists and Transatlantic Reform* (Baton Rouge: Louisiana State University Press, 2013); R. J. M. Blackett, *Building an Antislavery Wall: Black Americans in the Atlantic Abolitionist Movement* (Baton Rouge: Louisiana State University Press, 1983).

9. Eric Foner, *Free Soil, Free Labor, Free Men: The Ideology of the Republican Party before the Civil War*, 2nd ed. (New York: Oxford University Press, 1995), x–xi.

10. Christy Clark-Pujara, *Dark Work: The Business of Slavery in Rhode Island* (New York: New York University Press, 2016); Joanne Pope Melish, *Disowning Slavery: Gradual Emancipation and "Race" in New England, 1780–1860* (New York: Cornell University Press, 1998).

11. *Laws of State of North Carolina, Passed by the General Assembly, at the Session of*

1846–47 (Raleigh: Lemay, 1847), 109–13. See also Sylviane A. Diouf, *Slavery's Exiles: The Story of the American Maroons* (New York: New York University Press, 2014), 215.

12. R. J. M. Blackett, *The Captive's Quest for Freedom: Fugitive Slaves, the 1850 Fugitive Slave Law, and the Politics of Slavery* (New York: Cambridge University Press, 2018); Robert H. Churchill, "When the Slave Catchers Came to Town: Cultures of Violence along the Underground Railroad," *Journal of American History* 105, no. 3 (December 2018): 514–37.

13. William Craft and Ellen Craft, *Running a Thousand Miles for Freedom; or, The Escape of William and Ellen Craft from Slavery* (London: Tweedie, 1860); William Still, *The Underground Railroad Records* (Philadelphia: Porter and Coates, 1872); Henry Brown, *Narrative of Henry Box Brown, Who Escaped from Slavery, Enclosed in a Box 3 Feet Long and 2 Wide* (Boston: Brown and Stearns, 1849).

14. Gordon S. Barker, *The Imperfect Revolution: Anthony Burns and the Landscape of Race in Antebellum America* (Kent, Ohio: Kent State University Press, 2010).

15. Corey M. Brooks, *Liberty Power: Antislavery Third Parties and the Transformation of American Politics* (Chicago: University of Chicago Press, 2016); Robert F. Engs and Randall M. Miller, "The Genesis and Growth of the Republican Party: A Brief History," in *The Birth of the Grand Old Party: The Republicans' First Generation*, ed. Robert F. Engs and Randall M. Miller (Philadelphia: University of Pennsylvania Press, 2002), 1–7; William E. Gienapp, *The Origins of the Republican Party, 1852–1856* (New York: Oxford University Press, 1987).

16. Charles Sumner, *Crime against Kansas, the Apologies for the Crime, the True Remedy: Speech of Hon. Charles Sumner, in the Senate of the United States, 19th and 20th May, 1856* (Boston: Jewett, 1856); Williamjames Hull Hoffer, *The Caning of Charles Sumner: Honor, Idealism, and the Origins of the Civil War* (Baltimore: Johns Hopkins University Press, 2010); Manisha Sinha, "The Caning of Charles Sumner: Slavery, Race, and Ideology in the Age of the Civil War," *Journal of the Early Republic* 23, no. 2 (July 2003): 233–62.

17. Ted Maris-Wolf, *Family Bonds: Free Blacks and Re-enslavement Law in Antebellum Virginia* (Chapel Hill: University of North Carolina Press, 2015).

18. For more on slavery and freedom in Gates County, see Warren E. Milteer Jr., "Life in a Great Dismal Swamp Community: Free People of Color in Pre–Civil War Gates County, North Carolina," *North Carolina Historical Review* 91, no. 2 (April 2014): 144–70; Warren E. Milteer Jr., "The Strategies of Forbidden Love: Family across Racial Boundaries in Nineteenth-Century North Carolina," *Journal of Social History* 47, no. 3 (2014): 612–26.

19. Gates County, Miscellaneous Records, Slave Records, 1783–1867, n.d., SANC. The Gates County register has been transcribed and published as Raymond Parker Fouts, *Registration of Slaves to Work in the Great Dismal Swamp, Gates County, North Carolina, 1847–1861* (Cocoa, Fla.: GenRec, 1995).

20. Fouts, *Registration of Slaves*, 1–3.

21. Ibid., 1.

22. Ibid., February 24, 1852, 221.

23. Gates County, Miscellaneous Records, Slave Records; Proceedings of the Commissioners of the Town of Gatesville in 1833 and Gates County Registration of Slaves to Work in the Great Dismal Swamp, 1847–1861, 258, SANC.

24. Fouts, *Registration of Slaves*, July 19, 1854, 280.

25. Ibid., May 11, 1855, 294.

26. Ibid., September 20, 1856, 335. Daina Ramey Berry has recently pointed to the value that enslaved people held in all stages of a lifetime, from birth to death and even beyond, as enslaved peoples' bodies often formed the basis of early medical and anatomical experiments. See Daina Ramey Berry, *The Price for a Pound of Their Flesh: The Value of the Enslaved, from Womb to Grave, in the Building of a Nation* (Boston: Beacon, 2017).

27. Fouts, *Registration of Slaves*, September 24, 1857, 358.

28. Edmond Boothe certificate, September 1857, Gates County, Miscellaneous Records, Slave Records.

29. Tommy L. Bogger, *Free Blacks in Norfolk, Virginia, 1790–1860: The Darker Side of Freedom* (Charlottesville: University of Virginia Press, 1997), 1–3.

30. O. W. Flynn to Henry L. Eure, October 10, 1859, Gates County, Miscellaneous Records, Slave Records.

31. Porte Crayon [David Hunter Strother], *Osman the Maroon in the Swamp*, *Harper's New Monthly Magazine*, September 1856.

32. *Liberator*, December 30, 1842. See Henry Wadsworth Longfellow, *The Complete Poetical Works of Henry Wadsworth Longfellow* (Project Gutenberg, http://www.gutenberg .org/cache/epub/1365/pg1365.html).

33. Elizabeth R. Varon, *Disunion!: The Coming of the American Civil War, 1789–1859* (Chapel Hill: University of North Carolina Press, 2008); Leonard L. Richards, *The Slave Power: The Free North and Southern Domination, 1780–1860* (Baton Rouge: Louisiana State University Press, 2000).

34. Frederick Douglass, "The Heroic Slave," in *Autographs for Freedom*, ed. Julia Griffiths (Boston: Jewett, 1853), 174–239; William Wells Brown, *Clotel; or, The President's Daughter: A Narrative of Slave Life in the United States* (London: Partridge and Oakey, 1853); Martin R. Delany, *Blake; or, The Huts of America: A Corrected Edition*, ed. Jerome McGann (Cambridge: Harvard University Press, 2017).

35. Jonathan Earle and Diane Mutti Burke, eds., *Bleeding Kansas, Bleeding Missouri: The Long Civil War on the Border* (Lawrence: University Press of Kansas, 2013); Nicole Etcheson, *Bleeding Kansas: Contested Liberty in the Civil War Era* (Lawrence: University Press of Kansas, 2004).

36. Harriet Beecher Stowe, *Dred: A Tale of the Great Dismal Swamp*, ed. Robert S. Levine (New York: Penguin, 2000), ix–xxxv. For Stowe's biography, see Joan D. Hedrick, *Harriet Beecher Stowe: A Life* (New York: Oxford University Press, 1994).

37. Frederick Law Olmsted, *The Cotton Kingdom: A Traveller's Observations on Cotton and Slavery in the American Slave States*, ed. Arthur M. Schlesinger (New York: Knopf, 1953), 120–23; Frederick Law Olmsted, "The South: Letters on the Productions, Industry, and Resources of the Southern States, Number Thirteen," *New-York*

Daily Times, April 23, 1853. Journalist and antislavery activist James Redpath also visited the Lower Chesapeake, where he interviewed enslaved people. See James Redpath, *The Roving Editor; or, Talks with Slaves in the Southern States* (New York: Burdick, 1859), 291; John R. McKivigan, *Forgotten Firebrand: James Redpath and the Making of Nineteenth-Century America* (Ithaca: Cornell University Press, 2008).

38. Edmund Jackson, "The Virginia Maroons," *The Liberty Bell: By Friends of Freedom*, 1852, 143–51. Jackson's earlier work included "Effects of Slavery," *The Liberty Bell: By Friends of Freedom*, 1842, 39–43; "The Fugitive," *The Liberty Bell: By Friends of Freedom*, 1847, 5–15; "Servile Insurrections," *The Liberty Bell: By Friends of Freedom*, 1851, 158–64.

39. Andrew Kull, *The Color-Blind Constitution* (Cambridge: Harvard University Press, 1998).

40. Olmsted, *Cotton Kingdom*, 121.

41. Benjamin Quarles, *The Negro in the Civil War* (Boston: Little, Brown, 1953); James M. McPherson, *The Negro's Civil War: How American Blacks Felt and Acted during the War for the Union* (New York: Ballantine, 1991); Joseph T. Glatthaar, *Forged in Battle: The Civil War Alliance of Black Soldiers and White Officers* (New York: Meridian, 1991); Patricia C. Click, *Time Full of Trial: The Roanoke Island Freedmen's Colony, 1862–1867* (Chapel Hill: University of North Carolina Press, 2001); David S. Cecelski, *The Fire of Freedom: Abraham Galloway and the Slaves' Civil War* (Chapel Hill: University of North Carolina Press, 2012).

EPILOGUE. "FROM LOG CABIN TO THE PULPIT"

1. "Laboring under Misapprehensions," *Broad Ax*, May 16, 1899.

2. Correspondent Raymond, "The Negro in the South, Is Laboring under Misapprehension," *Chicago Tribune*, August 8, 1903.

3. Frederick Street, "In the Dismal Swamp," *Frank Leslie's Popular Monthly*, March 1903.

4. Waverley Traylor, *The Great Dismal Swamp in Myth and Legend* (Pittsburgh: Rosedog, 2010); Bland Simpson, *The Great Dismal: A Carolinian's Swamp Memoir* (Chapel Hill: University of North Carolina Press, 1990), 3–4.

5. William H. Robinson, *From Log Cabin to the Pulpit; or, Fifteen Years in Slavery*, 3rd ed. (Eau Claire, Wis.: Tifft, 1913); Kevin K. Gaines, *Uplifting the Race: Black Leadership, Politics, and Culture in the Twentieth Century* (Chapel Hill: University of North Carolina Press, 1996).

6. Robinson, *From Log Cabin to the Pulpit*, 24–25. Peter was a slave pilot at the Wilmington harbor; historian David Cecelski notes his interaction with William Robinson. See David S. Cecelski, *The Waterman's Song: Slavery and Freedom in Maritime North Carolina* (Chapel Hill: University of North Carolina Press, 2001), 121–23.

7. Robinson, *From Log Cabin*, 30.

8. Ibid., 28–38.

9. Ibid., 96–98, 117, 103–6. Robinson's experiences mirrored those of other enslaved African Americans thus impressed by the Confederates. See Bruce Levine, *Confed-*

erate Emancipation: Southern Plans to Free and Arm Slaves during the Civil War (New
York: Oxford University Press, 2006).

10. Robinson, *From Log Cabin*, 106–9, 122–25.

11. Ibid., 130–33, 134–35.

12. Ibid., 137, 146–50.

13. Ibid., 136–51, 158–59.

14. Ibid., 9.

15. Margot Minardi, *Making Slavery History: Abolitionism and the Politics of Memory
in Massachusetts* (New York: Oxford University Press, 2012); Grace Elizabeth Hale,
Making Whiteness: The Culture of Segregation in the South, 1890–1930 (New York: Pantheon, 1998); William C. Davis, *The Causes Lost: Myths and Realities of the Confederacy* (Lawrence: University Press of Kansas, 1996); John David Smith, *An Old Creed
for the New South: Proslavery Ideology and Historiography, 1865–1918* (Athens: University of Georgia Press, 1991); Eric Foner, *Reconstruction: America's Unfinished Revolution, 1863–1877* (New York: Harper and Row, 1988); C. Vann Woodward, *Origins of the
New South, 1877–1913* (Baton Rouge: Louisiana State University Press, 1971); Kenneth
M. Stampp, *The Era of Reconstruction, 1865–1877* (New York: Vintage, 1965).

16. W. E. B. Du Bois, *Black Reconstruction in America* (1935; New York: Atheneum,
1969); W. E. B. Du Bois, *The Souls of Black Folk* (1903; Boston: Bedford, 1997); John
Hope Franklin, *Reconstruction* (Chicago: University of Chicago Press, 1961).

See also Jeffrey R. Kerr-Ritchie, *Freedpeople in the Tobacco South: Virginia, 1860–
1900* (Chapel Hill: University of North Carolina Press, 1999); Joanne Pope Melish, *Disowning Slavery: Gradual Emancipation and "Race" in New England, 1780–1860*
(Ithaca: Cornell University Press, 1998); Leon F. Litwack, *Trouble in Mind: Black
Southerners in the Age of Jim Crow* (New York: Knopf, 1998).

17. David W. Blight, *Race and Reunion: The Civil War in American Memory* (Cambridge: Belknap Press of Harvard University Press, 2001), 438. Blight has argued that
the narrative is best characterized as "fictional history combined with a personal narrative" (438). Blight is struck by Robinson's use of Civil War imagery and place-names
throughout the narrative, a trope that would have resonated widely with audiences,
foregrounding the black freedom struggle as the nation commemorated the passage
of a half century since the end of the Civil War. Robinson's narrative was but one of
many publications aimed at promoting not only racial uplift, "a particularly African
American vision" (438) of progress in the years following slavery, but also a clear statement of the meaning that the African American community assigned to both the war
and emancipation.

18. Steven Hahn, *The Political Worlds of Slavery and Freedom* (Cambridge: Harvard
University Press, 2009), 24.

19. Neil Roberts, *Freedom as Marronage* (Chicago: University of Chicago Press,
2015).

INDEX

abolitionism: in Atlantic world, 38, 64; black activists for, 11, 88, 91, 107; colonization and, 5, 8, 52, 83, 88, 98; gag rule on, 91; Great Dismal Swamp and, 1, 2, 14, 64, 66, 90–93, 98–99; schism in, 92; slave conspiracy for, 48; slave trade and, 8; Virginia and, 10–11, 82–83

Abram (antislavery conspirator), 49, 51

Absalom (antislavery conspirator), 49, 51

Act Concerning Servants and Slaves (Virginia; 1705), 17

agency, 9, 10, 11, 101

Aichison, William: Atlantic trade of, 20–21, 22, 23–24; Campania Company and, 28; as Loyalist, 21; in slave trade, 21

Aichison and Parker firm, 24

Albert (enslaved swamp laborer), 96

Allmand, Harrison, 35

American Anti-Slavery Society, 91

American Colonization Society, 5, 8

American Revolution: DSC and, 28; Ethiopian Regiment in, 13, 19, 22; Loyalists and, 8, 13, 21; maroon role in, 18–19, 38; slavery and, 7; slave uprisings and, 12, 18, 38

Amos, Uncle (maroon watchman and prophet), 105, 108

Anderson, Jack, 95

Andrews, E. Benjamin, 81

Andrews, Robert, 30, 31, 37

Anthony (enslaved shingle getter), 85

Antigua, 29

antislavery movement. *See* abolitionism; slave conspiracies; slave uprisings

Aptheker, Herbert, 7

archival silence, 12, 21, 22, 29; on swamp general, 39

Atlantic world: abolitionist movement in, 38, 64; black agency in, 8, 10; black women in, 8; commodity trade and, 20–21, 22, 23–24, 41–42, 52, 57, 62, 63, 65, 74, 90, 92, 101; maroons in, 1–2, 7, 62, 108; slavery and, 7, 8, 40, 41–42, 91

Bacon, Anthony, 25

Baptist, Edward, 9

Bartee, John, 44, 61, 76

Bartee, Wilson, 61

Bear Quarter Company, 40, 43–48, 61, 71; Dismal Swamp Canal and, 55, 59–60; slave labor camp of, 44

Beckenworth, William S., 105

Beckert, Sven, 9–10

Bentoso, Francisco, 20

Berlin, Ira, 7

Berry, Daina Ramey, 9, 21

Blake (Delany), 98

Blight, David W., 139n17

Blow, Richard, 54, 57–58, 59, 62, 64

Bob (antislavery conspirator), 49, 51

Bob, Old (enslaved letter carrier), 54, 57, 65

Bogger, Tommy, 96

Bond, Lewis, 60

Booker, John, 48

Boothe, Edmond, 14, 94–96

Boush, Caleb, 51

Boykin, John, 80–81

Bracken, John, 47

Brickell, John, 5, 15

British Board of Trade, 4

British Empire. *See* American Revolution; Great Britain

Broad Ax, 103

CPSIA information can be obtained
at www.ICGtesting.com
Printed in the USA
LVHW091931290621
691478LV00001B/72